RETHINKING SEX

RETHINKING
Sex

— *a provocation* —

Christine Emba

SENTINEL

Sentinel
An imprint of Penguin Random House LLC
penguinrandomhouse.com

Most Sentinel books are available at a discount when purchased in quantity
for sales promotions or corporate use. Special editions, which include
personalized covers, excerpts, and corporate imprints, can be created
when purchased in large quantities. For more information, please call
(212) 572-2232 or e-mail specialmarkets@penguinrandomhouse.com.
Your local bookstore can also assist with discounted bulk purchases using
the Penguin Random House corporate Business-to-Business program.
For assistance in locating a participating retailer,
e-mail B2B@penguinrandomhouse.com.

Library of Congress Cataloging-in-Publication Data

Names: Emba, Christine, author.
Title: Rethinking sex : a provocation / Christine Emba.
Description: [New York] : Sentinel, [2022] | Includes bibliographical references. |
Identifiers: LCCN 2021054061 (print) | LCCN 2021054062 (ebook) |
ISBN 9780593087565 (hardcover) | ISBN 9780593087572 (ebook)
Subjects: LCSH: Sexual ethics. | Sex (Psychology)
Classification: LCC HQ31 .E734 2022 (print) | LCC HQ31 (ebook) |
DDC 176/.4—dc23/eng/20211110
LC record available at https://lccn.loc.gov/2021054061
LC ebook record available at https://lccn.loc.gov/2021054062

Printed in the United States of America
1st Printing

Book design by Jennifer Daddio

It is only by asserting one's humanness every time,
in all situations, that one becomes someone
as opposed to something. That, after all,
is the core of our struggle.

—ANDREA DWORKIN, *Woman Hating*

Contents

IN MY FRESHMAN YEAR of college, I started dating a junior. My friends had watched our artless flirtations across sticky beer pong tables and charted with interest our extended study sessions at the dimmest libraries around campus. One weekend night, after I'd been conspicuously absent from my undersized dorm room the evening before (for once, my long-suffering roommate was allowed to fall asleep without first enduring the two a.m. recitation of my interactions with the various "interesting" guys in our dining hall), my lewdest, drunkest friend smirked at me over a Solo cup sloshing with watery Milwaukee's Best.

"So," Jacob demanded, loudly enough to catch the interest of our underage bartender, who immediately began to listen in.

"Did you . . . *handle* . . . the peen?" The question was accompanied by a bizarre two-handed gesture akin to testing the casing of a giant sausage or fingering the keys of a clarinet. It stopped me in my tracks.

My friends and I burst into horrified laughter, which saved me the embarrassment of having to reply. No, I definitely had not been handling my new boyfriend's penis, and definitely not in the alarmingly visceral manner that was being implied. And I wouldn't, not for years.

THE AVERAGE AMERICAN millennial has their sexual debut around the age of seventeen. I came onstage more than a decade later than that: I was saving myself for marriage. I grew up an evangelical Christian, and converting to Catholicism in college— at a time when many of my similarly brought-up peers were leaning out of the traditionalist religions of their youth—cemented that decision, at least for several more years.

It's not that I didn't *want* to have sex in all that time—I did, sometimes desperately. I didn't escape my college's hookup scene untouched, and several boyfriends' worth of on-the-edge encounters left me (and them, I'm sure) furious at myself for my stance. I ran up against my commitments in narrow dorm bunk beds and on first-apartment mattresses laid on the floor, wrapped in the hot, rumpled sheets of those New York City summer nights that seemed made for the crush of bodies. My whispered *no*s left me feeling more and more outside the current as the years passed.

Despite my perpetual virginity, my non-sex-having twenties were full of sex, even if I wasn't the one having it. Countless brunch conversations revolved around my friends' experiences with the men and women in their lives and their processing of what every moment and movement meant. I was goggled at whenever I revealed my uneventful celibacy to a new friend and was frequently (and often reproachfully) lectured on how I was "missing out."

What I heard again and again was contradiction: Having sex was a marker of adulthood and a way to define yourself—but also, the act itself didn't really matter. Good sex was the consummate experience—but a relationship with your partner was not to be expected. It was nearly impossible not to indulge your desires, and extended celibacy was a state near unto death—yet I could and did say no and was clearly still alive.

I didn't end up waiting until marriage to have sex. I held on to my abstinence for a while and then let it go, after emerging from a failed relationship and wrestling with my own faith. I stayed Catholic, but sex went from something longed for and maybe slightly feared to something far more down-to-earth. Still, from my unusual vantage point—outside the postvirginal circle, then inside—the narratives around sex seemed deeply confused.

Maybe these stories sound familiar to you:

- Thinking that we should be having sex, even when we don't really desire it, because that's the impression society gives us—and thus seeing ourselves as incomplete, abnormal, or fallen behind if we aren't doing it, even when we're nothing of the sort.

- Having sex that we don't really want for reasons that we don't fully agree with far more often than we would like—but also thinking that that's just how it goes, and that it would be unreasonable to ask for more.

- Feeling jaded and discouraged by the romantic landscape, its lack of trust, emotion, and commitment—but also feeling as though other options aren't reachable or even realistic.

- Experiencing too much of the kind of sex that saps the spirit and makes us feel less human, not more— sex that leaves us detached, disillusioned, or just dissatisfied.

- Knowing that something in our sex and dating culture is somehow off, and wishing that things were different—even if we don't know exactly why we feel this way or how to make the shift to something better.

Hopes are high, outcomes trend low. Social expectations seem at odds with our true desires. And for something meant to bring pleasure, sex is causing a lot of pain.

It feels as though we have accepted many of these disappointments as normal—unfortunate but not criminal, the cost of doing business even after #MeToo. Yet things don't have to be criminal to be profoundly bad. And the fact that so many of the women around me relate so deeply to stories of harrowing dates and lackluster encounters shows that a lot of us are having a lot of *bad* sex. Unwanted, depressing, even traumatic: if this is ordinary, something is deeply wrong.

The goal of this book is to reassure you that *you're not crazy.* That the thing you sense is wrong *is* wrong. That there is something unmistakably off in the way we've been going about sex and dating.

Rather than suggesting marginal improvements to these problems, I'd like to ask you to rethink the assumptions beneath our approach to sex, the ones that got us here and the ones that add to our dissatisfaction. For instance: "Sex is a purely physical act." "The absence of rules will make me happier." "My sex life is nobody's business." "Women and men are basically the same."

What happens after we've identified the faulty assumptions? That's a more complicated project. I can make some suggestions—and I will make a fairly radical one—but I can't give you rules that will mean we never have to talk about this again. There's no simple, cut-and-dried, one-and-done approach to getting rid of bad sex. But there is a positive vision to reach for: a sexual culture that is pleasurable, connective, and enriching instead of confusing, alarming, or immiserating. And there are steps we can begin to take to get there: making substantive claims about what sex is and means that can be argued over, critiqued, and revised; moving past our laser focus on consent and discussing the other elements of ethical behavior that we've left by the wayside.

A quick note: This book deals with historical and cultural

ideas about sex, sexuality, and gender. As I try to describe why we should rethink sex, I should acknowledge that I am writing and thinking with mainly heterosexual relationships in mind. While these debates about sex are valid and important for those of all identities and orientations, cisgender heterosexuality is where our cultural scripts run deepest, and it is often in heterosexual relationships where they have the most gravitational force.

A rising share of the population identifies as gay, queer, or nonbinary, and I wish I had more to say to people who identify as such: I'm still learning. But even these relationships are often navigated within—or at least influenced by—the dominant sexual narrative and the ethics it implies. The arguments in this book may not apply to every sexual encounter. That said, I think that there is something for everyone here.

Rethinking Sex is not just about rethinking sex, the act. It is a rethinking of the way that we approach our bodies, our relationships, ourselves, and those around us. It's rethinking the possibility of what sex *could* be and raising our expectations. It's not just finding ways to prevent disappointment—it's finding out how to pursue joy.

You may agree with my conclusions, or you may not—either outcome is fine by me. But at least with some ideas on the table, we can start talking together about where to go next.

Let's rethink sex.

RETHINKING SEX

CHAPTER 1

Solving the Wrong Problem

SEPTEMBER 2006. I'm starting my freshman year of college. It's orientation, and it's time to talk about sex. We file into a dark auditorium to watch "Sex on a Saturday Night," a meant-to-be-educational skit that will show us how it all works here, in the fresh wilderness of dorms and parties and our new set of peers.

The loud buzz of chatter dies down as the curtain goes up. Upperclassman actors dramatize a typical weekend night out, complete with budding romances, bad jokes, and too much to drink. We crow with laughter. They show us a pregame, a party, and then—startlingly—an alcohol-enabled sexual assault.

Fade to black. We file out more quietly than we came in.

.   .   .

SEPTEMBER 2018. I'm no longer a student, but I'm visiting my college again, on a reporting assignment for my actual, adult job as an opinion columnist at *The Washington Post*. It's orientation, and the freshmen have to talk about sex. We file into a dark auditorium to watch a meant-to-be-educational skit that will show them how it all works here, in the fresh wilderness of dorms and parties and their new set of peers.

The loud buzz of chatter dies down as the curtain goes up. Upperclassman actors dramatize a typical weekend night out, complete with budding romances, bad jokes, and too much to drink. The crowd crows with laughter. They show us a pregame, a party, and then—startlingly—an alcohol-enabled sexual assault.

Fade to black. We file out more quietly than we came in. Over a decade later, very little has changed.

WHICH IS ODD, because in the real world quite a lot has happened.

In 2017 *The New York Times* publishes a blockbuster investigation into Hollywood film producer Harvey Weinstein, accusing him of raping, sexually assaulting, and sexually abusing dozens of women over the past thirty years. In the months that follow, a wave of similar stories begins to flood the news. Women have been suffering sexual misconduct for years, and they're fed up. Women are saying #MeToo, and people *believe them*. No one can look away. It feels like a reckoning may be taking place.

But the problem is not as simple, or as obvious, as bosses locking their underlings into hotel rooms.

Just a few months after the wave of highly public firings, *The New Yorker* publishes "Cat Person," a short story about two characters—Margot, a twenty-year-old college student, and Robert, a man in his midthirties—who go on a single bad date. Told in the third person but from Margot's perspective, it takes the reader through her thought processes as she realizes that she doesn't want to have sex with Robert but, for a variety of reasons, does so anyway. The story touches on the power imbalances of gender, the unpredictability of emotion, the commonness of unwanted sex, yet Margot's experience is not seen as particularly disastrous—it's more banal than anything else. And it seems to reflect the disappointing state of affairs that has somehow, maybe without our fully realizing it, come to be the new normal in sexual relations—at least for women. "Cat Person" goes viral because women around the country can relate. It's the most-read piece of online fiction *The New Yorker* has ever published.

And that piece of literary fiction is followed just a month later by its nonfiction mirror image on the website babe.net.

"I went on a date with Aziz Ansari," reads the headline. "It turned into the worst night of my life."

A young woman, pseudonym "Grace," recounts a date with the super popular, self-described-feminist comedian (who, incidentally, published a book on "modern romance" not more than eighteen months before the encounter took place). She describes his aggressive sexual advances and the feeling that she was being pressured into sex, despite her verbal and nonverbal expressions of discomfort. In the end, she goes along with it and eventually leaves in tears, feeling violated by Ansari's grotesque behavior.

It's real life, unlike "Cat Person," but it's another story that feels almost . . . ordinary? And for many of the 2.5 million readers who clicked on it in the twenty-four hours after its publication, Grace's grim indignity is painfully relatable.

"Throughout my high school and college years, I've listened helplessly as friends and acquaintances have described encounters with their own Azizs, and I've cried to them when I had my own," writes journalist Rebecca Alifimoff. "It's an ugly tapestry of close-calls and unwanted sexual encounters."

I didn't really want it, but I did it; it wasn't rape, but it feels bad.

In the meantime, the "Shitty Media Men" list emerges. The shared Google spreadsheet created by writer and editor Moira Donegan allows women to anonymously collate rumors and incidents of sexual misconduct by men in the magazine and publishing industry. But the offenses recorded run the gamut, from outright rape to the less obviously bad. Alongside the starkest allegations, there are accusations of "forced cuddling," "creepy DMs," "encourag[ing] other men to have sex with blacked out women because 'that's what they're there for.'" The solidarity of the document's creation is cathartic; the prevalence of sexual misconduct it reveals is shocking. Still, it marks a shift: The whisper network becomes concrete. Normal, not-famous women's complaints might finally be taken seriously. It feels, at least a little bit, like change is afoot.

BACK TO THE COLLEGE AUDITORIUM. Actually, in 2018, a few things about that hour in the auditorium *have* changed, perhaps because the #MeToo movement had spurred administrators into self-defensive action. "Sex on a Saturday Night" has been retitled—it's now "The Way You Move." (Still cringeworthy but less salacious.) And in 2018, there's a lengthy debrief immediately after the curtain falls. The main character having sex with a blacked-out classmate was not okay, an administrator explains, because the classmate could not consent. She goes to great lengths in discussing the "gray area" between a clear yes and an absolute no. It's a "contaminated" space, we hear, where to engage in sexual activity is to assume varying amounts of risk.

This was where the 2018 version of the play strikes me as odd, in a way it had not back when I was one of the eighteen-year-olds in the audience. The only real change to the production is that this year's debrief is all about consent: pedantically describing what part of the show's sex is legally problematic, and how to stay in the clear.

WHEN IT CAME to the headline #MeToo moments in 2017, the big stories tended to be black-and-white cases of nonconsent: "No doubt, Roy Moore/Kevin Spacey/Matt Lauer is a predator. Into the garbage he goes." But the later ones were not.

On the "Shitty Media Men" list, accounts of physical assault mingled with behavior that wasn't technically a crime. Sure, some of what these anonymous women describe wasn't great—but is anything other than "real" assault all that serious? What exactly rises to the level of "bad behavior"? What does that even mean?

Though there were plenty of missed or ignored cues in the babe.net story, as in "Cat Person," there's no clear nonconsent or violence. These were freely chosen, adult relationships—even if they took a dark turn by the end, even if they were experienced by their participants as exploitative or maybe even traumatic.

"I've definitely been in hookup relationships where there's no contact afterwards," twenty-four-year-old Melissa* told me. "And like, I'm not necessarily asking for anything like serious; we don't even have to put a label on it at that point. But at the same time, to engage in such an intimate act and then have the person just pretend you're not there is demoralizing. It makes you feel so . . . less than."

The unhappy stories my friends tell, the stories the college students and young adults I interview tell—these are not stories that are primarily about consent, about whether someone said yes loudly enough or had a clear no ignored. Rather, they're about care or the lack thereof, about the responsibilities we have to each other. They're about the gulf between the relationships that peo-

---

* Throughout this book, names and identifying details have been changed out of concern for privacy.

ple are seeking and the ones their social climate puts on offer. They're about what sex means—or at least, what it *should* mean.

WE TALK A LOT about sex—who's having it, how we should perform, what's appealing and what's a turnoff. And yet we rarely stop to think about the meaning of the act itself: what we believe that sex actually is, why we're having it, and what we want from it—what we are really looking for in our sexual, romantic, or dating lives.

Our shorthands—sex defined as the mechanical act of penetration, orgasms as something you give or get—oversimplify. They dumb sex down and make it smaller and meaner than what it could be. This is one of the reasons why consent—our shorthand for ethicality—so often falls short. Sex is complex; consent treats it like a problem of arithmetic.

In the essay "Does Anyone Have the Right to Sex?" Amia Srinivasan deconstructs a typically simplistic analogy used to illustrate the theory of consent. "'You don't get to have sex with someone unless they want to have sex with you,'" she writes, quoting from Rebecca Solnit's (otherwise brilliant) essay "Men Explain *Lolita* to Me," "'just as 'you don't get to share someone's sandwich unless they want to share their sandwich with you.'"

It's an obviously poor analogy, and the Oxford philosopher points out that it and others of its type—equating sex to meals, handshakes, or other quotidian objects—don't really hold up under scrutiny. "Sex is not a sandwich," Srinivasan writes, ". . . and it isn't really like anything else, either. There is nothing else so riven with politics and yet so inviolably personal. For better or worse, we must find a way to take sex on its own terms."

So what are those terms? Sandwiches are isolated, fungible objects, purposed as fuel and destined to exit unceremoniously from the nether end of one's digestive tract. At its best, the creation of the sandwich might convey the sandwich maker's affection. But as a general rule, sandwiches are as empty of meaning as they might be full of jam. They are made to be consumed and then forgotten. Sex, on the other hand, is something qualitatively different, and Srinivasan intuits that it should be treated and talked about as such.

"Sex is not a sandwich." It's a statement so obvious as to be almost absurd. Most of us sense—however dimly, as clouded as our imagination might be with analogies to bases in baseball, petals plucked from roses, or notches on belts—that our sexuality isn't an isolated behavior. Rather, it is tightly intertwined with our emotions and values, our personal history, and our physical being. Sex is a bodily function, but it involves the spirit, too. It implicates the human person and thus our inherent human dignity, which should lead us to treat it with a commensurate level of consideration—to acknowledge it as it is, with everything that could mean.

In 1982, during the waning days of the sexual revolution, feminist journalist Ellen Willis wrote: "Sexual liberals have promoted the competing assumption that sex is simply a healthy, enjoyable biological function with no intrinsic moral connotations. But this bland view not only violates most people's sense that their sexuality is not an isolated 'function,' . . . it also evades the question of sexual destructiveness."

Mind, Body, Soul . . . Other?

So what does it mean, then? We shouldn't overlook the obvious: A lot of what we like about sex is how it feels, and the best sex *feels really good.* Vital, even—one of the most intense human drives. "I love being fully in my body, the physical release," one woman told me. The modern understanding of sex holds that the desire to sleep with someone is the desire to engage in a very specific physical pleasure—the thrill of arousal, the physical abandonment of orgasm, the catharsis of a desire fulfilled. The underlying purpose of sex, biologically, is procreation, the continuance of the species. But sometimes the point of a particular encounter is just fun and feelings, a grown-up form of play.

But the physical pleasure that is so much of our sexual desire depends on a particular feature of sex—its embodied character. And *that* relies in large part on the fact that sex allows, and in fact requires, you to *touch* someone else. And it's skin-to-skin contact of a particularly thorough kind. A phenomenon frequently noted by psychologists—and better understood by the rest of us after months of coronavirus isolation—is skin hunger, the biological need for human touch. It's why babies in neonatal intensive care units are placed on their parents' naked chests and why unmothered children living in orphanages would sometimes wither away and die. Physical contact releases the hormone oxytocin, which aids in person-to-person bonding and reduces levels of the stress hormone cortisol. Being touched makes us feel happier, calmer, and more sane.

Psychotherapist and bestselling author Lori Gottlieb thinks that this factor is underrated in our considerations of why we have sex, especially for people in their twenties and thirties. As she told me in an interview, "Young people don't get touched very much unless they're having sex. And sometimes—it's especially hard for men to acknowledge this—it's not so much the sex, but it's that someone is hugging them and holding them. . . . It's that we're sleeping together and waking up together. And there's a warm body here with me."

But sex is something more than just a hug, a handshake, or even a sleepover. It's *intimacy*. Having sex, you are as naked and intertwined as you can be with another person—in a literal sense. There is a particular vulnerability there, of a kind that we rarely experience. After all, sex is sort of grotesque. It's a physical, biological function that can be kind of . . . ugly. We make faces. Our bodies make noises. We sweat, sigh, and emit fluids. In a supposedly advanced society, we don't share most of those things with other people. But when having sex, we have the rare opportunity to see each other bare, in ways that we rarely do otherwise.

And sometimes, when all the stars and body parts align, transcendence is possible. In the twenty-first century, most people no longer rely on religion to take them outside of themselves, to give them a taste of timelessness or infinity. But sex sometimes has elements of both.

You don't have to be a tantric guru to have come to this conclusion. One buttoned-up lawyer confessed, "To me, sex is almost . . . It can be like leaving the body, sort of, almost an escape. When you're so close to someone that you're almost out of your body—it can be almost disorienting. It's like the only time when something can almost take you outside of time and space."

An otherwise down-to-earth political activist said: "I consider myself somebody who kind of cares about the world quite a bit. Then I meet somebody and have great sex with them. And all of a sudden I'm, like, holed up in a room and the world could be burning outside and I have no idea. I think that it's just, like . . . a way to completely escape the world."

Sex may not necessarily feel like an out-of-body experience, but it can feel like something larger than yourself. When we make that connection with the right person, fulfill that particular desire, it sometimes leads to a near-spiritual experience, an escape outside of oneself. This experience of the sublime was one I heard again and again, from both women and men. The erotic can open us up, peeling away our protective layers and leaving us beautifully and wonderfully open to the world; sex can bring us beauty and restoration and awe. Most sexual encounters are not described as spiritual experiences—though a surprising number are—but there may be something of the mystical there, too.

There are sundry less exalted aspects, of course. Having sex can make you feel desirable and validated. It can be a venue for self-expression or exploration. Sex offers the possibility for us to exercise power over each other, or to revel in our own control.

Having sex can be proof that we're attractive enough to sleep with, proof that the other person likes us enough to open up, proof that we're adventurous or adult. We smooth over hurt feelings, humor our partners. Sometimes we're just acting out a role.

In some ways, sex is a paradox. It's the experience that situates us most completely in our bodies and the world, but it can also be the experience that gives us our sharpest taste of something beyond it. And often a sense of *something more* is what we really desire.

Consent Lessons

Today consent is the legal standard for good sex. Rape has been defined as "sex without consent" in twelve European countries.* Affirmative consent, once seen as the mockable obsession of overly progressive college campuses,† has now been written into law in five U.S. states. K–12 sex educators are urged to begin talking about consent in early childhood, and the most progressive parenting websites give advice for teaching the concept to babies (ask their permission before you change their diaper!). At colleges, students are force-fed consent education via eye-glazing training modules, posters plastered on every

---

* In Spain the sexual offense law is even called "Only Yes Means Yes" ("Solo sí es sí").

† The entire concept was ridiculed: A 1993 *Saturday Night Live* skit mocked it with a game show manned by sex-hating "victimization studies" majors. Dave Chappelle was still roasting the idea of a "love contract" in 2004.

available surface, and phalanxes of earnest "sexual health educators": modern-day pamphleteers. By the time you reach adulthood, it's simply common knowledge: consent is what you must obtain, legally, before you take part in a sexual encounter.

On many levels, this is a victory. It took a great deal of effort to get us to the place where consent is seen as a baseline requirement.

The earliest written rape law emerged around 1750 BC, in the Code of Hammurabi. It dictated that if a man forced sex on another man's wife or a virgin "living in her father's house," he should be put to death. It reflected the historically common view that rape was primarily a form of theft or vandalism; that the woman was the property of the father or husband, whose honor might be harmed.

Even as laws were slowly rewritten to recognize rape as a crime against the woman herself, the burden remained on her to prove her truthfulness, chastity, and resistance to attack—casting women as liars and making cases extraordinarily difficult to prosecute. (And this was for the women who were even seen as such—in the Southern United States, it wasn't until 1861 that a Black slave could even file charges of rape against a white man.)

In the 1970s, the feminist antirape movement organized speak-outs, hosted forums, and established rape crisis centers, drawing attention to the pervasiveness of sexual assault and violence against women. Still, the law didn't criminalize a man raping his spouse or "voluntary sexual partner" until the late 1970s. Donald Trump was bragging about grabbing women by the pussy in 2005 and won a presidential election in 2016 despite that fact. Laws that protected husbands who raped their wives from being prosecuted for sexual violence were still on the books in 2019.

"No means no" was a radical slogan when it was first popularized in the 1990s by the Canadian Federation of Students and the idea of affirmative consent—getting verbal permission clearly and often during a sexual encounter—was only implemented in 1991 at Antioch College, a tiny liberal arts school. "Enthusiastic consent" is an even more recent coinage, but it's already entering the mainstream lexicon. We've come a long way.

And yet the problems remain. It's not that students aren't learning their lessons about consent. It's that there are other lessons to learn.

The baseline norm is correct: Consent must be present in any sexual encounter; otherwise it is morally illegitimate. Having sex with someone who hasn't agreed to have sex with you is unacceptable; criminal, in fact.

But will more lectures on consent dissolve gender stereotypes, rebalance power differentials, explain intimacy, or teach us how to care? Reminding people to make sure they have consent becomes a case of providing a right answer to the wrong problem. And an overreliance on verbal consent might actually worsen this malaise: if you're playing by the rules and everything is still awful, what are you supposed to conclude?

"I DON'T KNOW," Rachel said with a gusty sigh. We were drinking iced coffees on an unseasonably warm October day. My twenty-five-year-old former colleague and I had both reflexively made fun of ourselves for our orders, but we also admitted that they did provide an outsize amount of joy.

"I've never been in a situation where I felt pushed into something, exactly, but . . . there have been times when I felt like, 'Oh, we're already here. We're already in my bed.' So I'll give them a blow job. Or I've gone home with someone and we're having sex and they keep asking for anal, or they say weird stuff to me—'You're a little slut, you're a bitch,' and I don't like it but it's like: this is the situation we're in, and I kind of feel like we have to . . . follow suit. It's not like I was being forced into anything or that I feel unsafe, but it's not . . . good. And I don't like how I feel afterwards."

She stirred her coffee with a finger and then licked it meditatively. "But you know, one of my coworkers mentioned that 'Cat Person' story to me at an internship. She said, 'Every single person I know—every woman I know—has had some questionable encounter, whether it was, like, really violent or really forceful or just kind of like, 'Oh, I hated that. That was not fun.'"

How do we respond to stories like these? We can say that the consent wasn't sufficient and try to get more or better consent. But is that the real problem here?

Over the past two decades, realization that the consent-based ethic wasn't always getting the job done has prompted attempts at refinement: simple consent was no longer enough; one now needed to get *the right kind*. In the mid-aughts, consensus moved away from "no means no" as the right consent formulation and coalesced around "yes means yes" instead. This phrase, and the accompanying idea of affirmative consent, made it clear that the absence of a *no* wasn't enough to constitute agreement, that the presence of a *yes* was needed, too. Rather than focusing on refusal—a negative response to badgering or unwanted attempts—it tried to turn the focus to enjoyment. "Yes" would ideally make the act of giving consent positive, turning it into an informed, empowering exchange.

More recently, the discourse has moved toward "enthusiastic" consent. More than the absence of a *no* and the presence of a *yes*, the *yes* needs to be engaged, excited, and active. This approach tries to distinguish between wanted and unwanted sex, even though both might conceivably be "consented" to, and attempts to encompass both agency and desire. And yet even here, I'm not sure that this has made much of a difference against the unhappiness that has come to light. The same complaints still repeat, and the same confusions still arise.

Consider the challenge of determining whether the right sort of consent is present in some situations: If a movie star deigns to sleep with an avid fan, are both engaging in an encounter of equals? If men and women have different fertility timelines, does that affect the power dynamic? What if one person is seeking a relationship and the other is not?

Even the newer, qualified versions of consent—the "affirmative," the "enthusiastic," still have that as their baseline question: "Did I get permission of the right *kind*, so that what I am going to do to this person is not statedly against their will?" The modifiers may try to complicate the question, but they're most often perceived as simply shifting the goalposts—rather than stopping when your partner says no, you now have to get them to say yes. But the end goal is still to Get the Sex from someone else without having committed an actual violation. If we invoke just getting consent as an ideal—*the* ideal, the highest ethical standard for any encounter—we're giving ourselves a pass on the hard but meaningful questions: whether that consent was fairly gotten, what our partners actually want, whether we even should be doing what we've gotten consent to do.

Even if we got consent right every single time, we might still have these questions—and no clear way to answer them. Because in the end, consent is a legal criterion, not an ethical one. While it is a necessary statutory framework and an excellent tool for risk avoidance, it doesn't address the questions that have become all the more pressing since #MeToo began. What are we talking about when we talk about sex? What does it mean, to us and to each other?

Nonconsensual sex is always wrong. But the inverse is tricky: Is consensual sex always right? Not necessarily. Can consensual sex be damaging to an individual, to their partner, to society? Absolutely. It's hard to look at the woes of our sexual "marketplace" and say that we've got it figured out. Consent is a fig leaf, and it's falling off.

This is not a popular thing to say. As a society we tend to shy away from declaring certain behaviors intrinsically wrong, or right, or uncomfortably in between. This may be done out of a skewed sense of pluralism: we've seen moral standards used to silence and discriminate and prefer not to cast further judgment.

Less attractively, it's done because we hate the idea of limiting ourselves: if we declare that something is always wrong, we might not be able to do certain things that we want to do. More frighteningly, perhaps, it would mean that we must sometimes do things that we would not prefer. The idea that sex might be meaningful and have consequences seems almost offensive, an affront to our liberation.

Right now, the broad agreement seems to be that sex is good, and the more of it we have, the better. We can have whatever kind of sex we want to have and do whatever we need to get it. There's only one rule: get consent for whatever you're about to do from your partner beforehand.

Except most of us aren't looking for *just* sex, or more of it, and that's why the broad agreement isn't working. What we are all looking for is a good life—ideally, for most of us, with good sex as part of it. When I say "good" I don't just mean pleasurable—although hopefully it is. I mean sex that is ethically good. Sex that respects us as human persons. Sex that is just—meaning noncoercive and taking into account our individual realities. Sex that puts the ideal sexual encounters that we hope for within reach and in fact validates those ideals as worthy goals. Sex that's good for society, our partners, *and* ourselves.

Making the standard of consent our sole criterion for good sex, we punt on the question of how to conduct a relationship that is not only allowable but also *right*—one that affirms us in our existence as sovereign human beings of intrinsic worth, and that is engaged in with our human dignity in mind.

And an ethic that makes consent the only rule doesn't account for how our actions are constrained by biology, by society, by norms that we did not choose. It doesn't address our fundamental personhood, the fact that events resonate within us long after the deeds are done. It doesn't ask what, if anything, we owe to each other. It doesn't tell us what behavior is right or wrong or what values should inform how we treat each other.

To find answers to these questions, we have to start making substantive claims about what we believe about sex, if only so they can be considered, critiqued, and revised to eventually get to something approaching the truth.

Because our frame of reference matters. To build something different, we have to acknowledge the reality of where we are. And if a new standard for behavior—or any other solution that we land upon—is based on false assumptions, we can expect the results of our efforts to be lackluster, too.

BACK TO THAT college auditorium.

After the presentation ended and the freshmen had filed out, I sneaked backstage to talk to a few of the student actors. What did *they* think of the play they'd just put on? Hadn't it seemed a little . . . incomplete?

"Yeah," shrugged one junior. To her, it had been painfully simplistic. "Do this, not that. Don't break the rules. But given the time constraints . . ."

She was right, of course. A one-hour tableau put together by college risk managers was never going to fully explain sex or impart a full understanding of human dignity, and it shouldn't have to. The ability to view relationships as shared, rather than transactional, to see other people as deserving of respect and goodwill—that's the work of decades.

But most of us don't have that kind of formation, at least when it comes to our sex lives. What understanding we do have has been shaped by an ideal of liberation, with personal agency as the key that unlocks every door. It's not a moral question, we tell ourselves: the problem with sex is gender roles, or social stigma, or a restrictive biological clock, or even our own unruly emotions that make consent confusing and speaking up harder than it should be. If we could just get really, truly free, things would be better.

But sex *has* become more liberated, by leaps and bounds. And the problems haven't gone away.

CHAPTER 2

We're Liberated, and We're Miserable

"YOU'RE GONNA HEAR a lot of man-bashing here," says Gayathri, a thirty-four-year-old law student from Maryland, smiling ruefully as we slide into an oversize booth. The lights are dim enough in this bar that you could be forgiven for not realizing you had stepped inside out of the night, were it not for the sounds of "I Love Rock 'n Roll" reverberating, strident and overloud, off the dark-painted walls.

"I almost hate men. Not almost." She laughs. "I do. At this stage, I've just stopped thinking a relationship is even possible." Gayathri is an animated speaker—she leans in to make her points with dark eyes flashing, every word sharply pronounced.

Over cocktails, she details her repeated encounters with men whom she describes as lacking the initiative to be reliable partners, because sex is both so casual and so available. "We had sex and would talk for hours, were in touch constantly, and then he disappeared for two weeks. I was like, 'What the hell happened to you?'"

Her description of what passes for a dating scene mingles comedy with despair. "My last good relationship was five years ago. And ever since then it's been these"—she throws her hands up in the air—"these *bullshit shenanigans*."

"I cannot settle anymore, for the in-between. I refuse," she says with a vehemence that surprises me. "And I'll be alone for the rest of my life, but I just . . . I cannot waste any more energy."

Viewed from the vantage point of, say, fifty years ago, it would look like women have reached an apex of sexual freedom. And in many ways, we are more unfettered when it comes to sex than ever before: less risk, less stigma, more opportunity, more options. So why are so many of us so dissatisfied?

"THE SHARE OF AMERICANS who say sex between unmarried adults is 'not wrong at all' is at an all-time high," reported *The Atlantic* journalist Kate Julian in 2018. "New cases of HIV are at an all-time low. Most women can—at last—get birth control for free, and the morning-after pill without a prescription."

She went on to list a cascade of other supposedly positive indicators: "If hookups are your thing, Grindr and Tinder offer the prospect of casual sex within the hour. . . . *Polyamory* is a household word. Shame-laden terms like *perversion* have given way to cheerful-sounding ones like *kink*. Anal sex has gone from final taboo to 'fifth base'—*Teen Vogue* (yes, *Teen Vogue*) even ran a guide to it."

The conclusion? "With the exception of perhaps incest and bestiality—and of course nonconsensual sex more generally—our culture has never been more tolerant of sex in just about every permutation."

Yet far from having achieved a sexual renaissance, the leading sex research journals consistently find that people are having sex *less* frequently than they used to. Young adults (in their twenties and early thirties) are more likely to be celibate in adulthood, and are on track to have fewer sexual partners over the course of their lives than Gen Xers or even their boomer parents. Julian's article dubs it the "sex recession."

We've breached the ramparts of repression, and the wall of silence that prevented us from expressing our sexuality has fallen. According to our expressed preference for liberation, this should make us happy. Openness is good! Freedom of choice is even better! We've gone from being penned in to being free to roam. But in the open field that now rolls out before us, everyone feels a bit . . . lost.

Heteropessimism

One of the first signs that something is amiss is the distress with which both men and women—though straight women especially—have come to regard the process of dating. The not-totally-in-jest jokes about the horrors of the opposite sex have always existed. But in the past they more often referred to marriage, the dustbin where the fire of dating supposedly went to die—not to the hopeful period before the flames were even lit.

If in the midaughts a thousand flowers of performative misandry bloomed (remember that purer, gentler time, when the internet overflowed with "Ban Men" cross-stitch and "MALE TEARS" mugs?), post-#MeToo, the declaration that *men are trash* has gone from goofy in-joke to exhausted lament. The optimistic premise of *The Bachelor* ("Once upon a time, twenty-five women met the man of their dreams. Unfortunately, they all met him on the same night.") has been eclipsed by the resigned disappointment of *FBOY Island*. (HBO decided to stylize the term *fuck boy*—a guy who strings you along but blows you off and doesn't treat you with respect—for mass consumption.) The 1990s bestseller *The Rules* was grimly prescriptive, but 2019's *How to Date Men When You Hate Men* is openly hostile.

Not all women want a male romantic partner. But for many of those who do, their ability to fulfill that desire seems to have dwindled. And in the present moment, the female outlook has come to take on a less playful, more depressive tone—what writer Indiana Seresin defines as "heteropessimism," a mode of feeling "usually expressed in the form of regret, embarrassment, and hopelessness about the straight experience." It's an anesthetic posture, one meant to help distance its mostly female adherents from really feeling a sense of sorrow for their lack of control and repeated disappointments, or from fully acknowledging the pervasive awfulness of a culture that's not suited to their happiness.

There's not an obvious fix. But having decided that the culture of heterosexual relationships no longer seems set up to get them what they want—interest, intimacy, relationships of trust—women are seeking other options.

Some have begun to rely more on their platonic relationships rather than expect much of value from the opposite sex. "I have tons of friends, like, very deep friendships with women," said Michelle, who felt that she was still processing the trauma of an ostensibly consensual sexual encounter. "And pretty much all my friends *don't* give me is sex and the intimacy of a [romantic] relationship." Is that enough? Maybe for now, at least—she was skeptical of dating as a solution. "I don't need more people who are not going to commit to me but want a lot of my brain space."

The memoir *Everything I Know About Love* runs through British writer Dolly Alderton's disastrous dates and absurd romantic encounters to conclude that only her best female friendships have stood the test of time, a conclusion that resonated strongly enough with readers to sell more than 300,000 copies in the UK alone. "Nearly everything I know about love, I've learnt in my long-term friendships with women," she wrote. "This kind of love might not kiss you in the rain or propose marriage. But it will listen to you, inspire and restore you. . . . Keep it as close to you as you can."

Other women have responded by giving up on the opposite

sex altogether, or at least being tempted to. I was surprised, in my interviews, by the number of women who told me that they either wished they were lesbians or had begun, if within their ability, to actively choose against men.

In college, Nora had a nonconsensual encounter with a class-mate at a party. It made headlines on her Ivy League campus and set her off on a multimonth period of drunken sexual en-counters to reclaim the feeling that "I could do that, and it could be good, and fun, and what I wanted to do."

Now twenty-three, she identifies as bisexual. She told me that she thought the stereotypes of women swearing off all men after one bad or questionable encounter were clichéd and harm-ful, and that that wasn't what had happened to her. But on the other hand, she acknowledged: "Most of the—not just romantic relationships, but most of the sexual relationships I've had since were with women or nonbinary people, not with men."

Nora stops to correct herself. "I mean, I *have* had sex with men, but not . . . very few, compared to the sexual relationships I've had with women and nonbinary people. And I think that is intentional? I'm afraid of saying that because I think it sort of makes real this harmful stereotype. But I also think that, like, I genuinely feel safer when I'm with people who aren't men. Basi-cally it's like men hurt us too much to even risk it, at this point."

It's a throwback to the radical feminist separatists of the 1970s and '80s, who viewed the patriarchy as inescapable and men as unfixable and saw total disengagement from them (via lesbian-ism or abstention or other modes of rejecting the institution of heterosexuality) as the only path to safety. "[As lesbian separatists] we believe that the first and most basic step necessary to attend to ourselves and our safety as women in the present world is to separate from men to the extent that that is possible," wrote noted separatist Jackie Anderson in 1994. It's apparently no longer such a radical idea.

And others are beginning to grapple with what it might look like to stay single, for much longer than they had hoped.

BACK IN THAT DARK BAR, Gayathri adds: "Boys just feel so underwhelming. It's really hard to meet somebody that you have a genuine connection with. And when you do, then that's far more fragile. You don't want to just jump in, and it's really hard to even find that space to build trust.

"I feel very alone in this, even though when I talk to some friends, the thing they'll say is 'I hear this from so many women.' It's comforting and not comforting at the same time, because it doesn't really solve any of my problems, and I don't see this about to change culturally. How women are emotionally trying to deal with the idea of being alone is, like, frightening and sad and overwhelming at times." She laughs rather wistfully. "I've come to realize that more and more I just don't want to sleep with somebody unless it's serious. But how am I ever going to get there with anybody?

"How do you really deal with that kind of loneliness? Or just being alone?"

.   .   .

HETEROPESSIMISM IS BY no means limited to women. Men express it too, although Seresin's points suggest that their claims "tend to be neither ethically nor logically equivalent to those made by women," and their complaints seem less terminal than the ones I hear from their female counterparts.

In her essay, Seresin highlights "incels," short for "involuntary celibates"—men who have come to define themselves by their inability to find a sexual or romantic partner. They gather in online forums to trade their tales of woe—or in some cases take out their anguish through mass shootings: UC Santa Barbara killer Elliot Rodger was one. Parkland shooter Nikolas Cruz was another. In Canada, Alek Minassian drove a van onto a crowded Toronto sidewalk, killing ten people and injuring sixteen more.

They're not exactly a sympathetic bunch, believing as they do that sex is something they're owed by women. Their difficulty in connecting with the opposite sex has turned into a personality-warping obsession. But at the base of their disconnect lies a grain of relatability: sex and relationships *are* meaningful. It is painful to feel, as the incels seem to, that connection is something everyone else is having without them. (In a 2019 Pew Research Center survey, men were twice as likely as women to say that they weren't dating because they thought that no one would be interested in dating *them*.)

The incels are an extreme, and perhaps their reactions are less related to a frustration with the current culture than a response to changing gender dynamics in society overall. (As women have gained much more choice and the ability to refuse men's attentions, backlash from men—stripped of their privilege as deciders—is the response.)

For a rather less toxic set of men, there's an overinternalization of the pessimistic attitudes they overhear, and the observed fallout from the #MeToo moment. Some might have been sensitive to potential romantic partners' feelings before, to the point of being afraid of overstepping boundaries. But now, as one woman put it, "these guys are just . . . not flirting, not even asking anyone out—not doing anything. They're just paralyzed with fear." A therapist I spoke to in New York City concurred: "Men in their twenties are terrified, and they talk about it a lot."

David, a twenty-nine-year-old software analyst living in San Francisco, put it in startling terms: He described making romantic overtures as "like handing someone a loaded shotgun or something. I mean, most people will be fine with it, but . . ." Better to stay safe, even if it means staying by yourself.

Dominic, a thirty-five-year-old consultant in DC, admitted: "I never was good at just, like, flirting with someone on the street or at a coffee shop." But now, he says, holding up his hands to signal his withdrawal, "I would never just approach a woman sitting by herself at a coffee shop. I feel like that's . . . it's kind of an aggressive move in these current circumstances. I almost never see it. You stay in your lane."

You could read this as a good thing, at least in some ways: it's great that men are being more conscious of what they say or do. But the flip side is that most men *aren't* rapists, and many women would eventually like to be approached by a potential partner. In different ways, both genders have lost confidence in their ability to be together—they no longer know how to do it correctly, or if it's even possible. They're giving up on the potential for a relationship and finding themselves alone.

"I DON'T THINK older generations realize how TERRIFY-ING dating is for the current generation. There is no commitment, everyone talks about 'let's see where this goes', there are no labels. Absolutely chaotic out here for people looking to get married," fumed @tishray on Twitter. The sentiment was reshared over four thousand times and garnered almost twenty thousand likes.

According to the Pew Research Center, nearly half of American adults say that dating has gotten harder for most people over the past ten years, with the actual dating population—the 15 percent or so of adults who are single and looking for a committed relationship or even just casual dating—saying that they are dissatisfied with their dating lives and that it has been difficult to find people to date. Fully half of single adults have given up on looking for a relationship or dating at all.

It makes sense, then, that in less than twenty years, the proportion of never-married Americans rose from 21 percent to 35 percent, a fourteen-point increase, and that the marriage rate among twenty-five- to thirty-four-year-olds in the U.S. declined thirteen percentage points in thirteen years. Pew went on to project that if current trends continue, cne in four of today's young adults may never marry.

But connection with others brings meaning to our lives, and loneliness kills—literally, as research has revealed. And durable romantic connection—not the stuff of fleeting hookups but the sort that has the potential to expand and create families, children, an extended clan—is often the most generative and meaningful of all.

The Worst Dinner Party

One major problem with "liberated" sex: without norms or boundaries, we don't know where things will stop—so we're afraid to start at all.

At the height of the #MeToo movement in the fall of 2017, a poll conducted by *The Economist* found that more than one in ten young American women (and one in four young men) thought that "asking [a woman] to go for a drink" would constitute sexual harassment.

It's an absurd number, especially considering the number of people who say that they wish that they could meet romantic partners through in-person connection rather than online or through an app.

But I would guess that part of the reason why at least some of those respondents believe being asked for a drink to be potential sexual harassment is not because they dislike being asked out but because they think it's likely that that's not where the inter-action is going to end.

If "being asked for a drink" could turn back into "being asked for a drink," not "being asked for a drink with the expectation that it will end in a sexual encounter" (or that it will be interpreted as such and thus rejected or even reported), such interactions would become much less fraught and much more pleasant, with much more potential to build into something great. But with sex gener-ally understood to always be on the table and the etiquette around it unclear, genuinely low-stakes, positive encounters feel more and more out of reach.

"ONE OF THE MOST IMPORTANT pleasures of sexual intimacy," according to Washington University professor and ethicist Fan-nie Bialek, whom I spoke to just a few days after my conversation with Gayathri, is "the good of feeling like you have the possibil-ity of the unexpected, but not *too much* possibility of the unex-pected."

Boundaries, as any therapist would tell you, are actually good. By defining the scope of what isn't wanted, they lay out a space for everything else that might be. What are the expecta-tions of a first date? What does having sex actually signify, and what should a first encounter look like? What can I expect to happen afterward? Are there things that we can fairly expect to be off limits, and can we trust that others will follow those rules?

As Dr. Bialek and I talked about what boundaries might look

like in a modern, sexually liberated world, she went on to use the analogy of a dinner party. "I pretty much know what's going to happen when I go to a dinner party. And the fact that unexpected things happen in the course of the conversation is pleasurable, because the unexpected can be pleasurable. But it's within a fairly tight boundary, in such a way that I don't feel shaken out of my comfort zone all the time."

To a greater or lesser extent, the same sort of intimacy with a touch of possibility is what people enjoy about flirtation and later hope to experience in their sexual encounters and even relationships. You go to dinner parties with new friends in part because you hope—although you can never be sure—that the person next to you might be fascinating and fun; that in conversation they will shock or delight you or teach you something new. In sexual and romantic encounters, that same pleasure of possibility is present in its most heightened form: you wonder whether the person across from you likes you, will kiss you, what they're thinking in the same moment, whether they'll bring you to ecstasy later that night or even change your life forever.

These days, however, one of those settings—the bedroom, not the dinner party—seems far more fraught than the other.

"Part of what is pleasurable about the norm regulation of dinner is that I can focus on the variations and the unexpected without being stressed," Dr. Bialek said. "I can be interested in the thing that someone says instead of worrying that they will stab me with a dinner knife. Not having to worry about all of these radically unexpected things frees up that attention and that possibility of enjoyment. But that's an aspect of sex that is really difficult. We want the unexpected within it, but we also need forms of safety that can structure the encounter."

That enjoyment of dinner parties rests upon a clear set of rules: a strong set of openly discussed, broadly shared, community-regulated norms for how all attendees should behave. Social norms are critical to our enjoyment of that sort of intimacy because they are what structure the delightful unexpected.

But in Professor Bialek's work as a sex educator and counselor, she has found that "people experience a lot more unexpected interaction in a sexual context than they do at dinner." Because of our unwillingness to acknowledge a shared set of norms for sex beyond the bare minimum of consent, the safe structure that allows us room to really experience the pleasure of the uncertain is often lacking in our romantic encounters, if not missing entirely.

Sex could be a delightful space of possibility. But without limitations, we're too worried to really enjoy ourselves.

How Did We Get Here?

Writing about a resurgence of interest in the famously polarizing feminist Andrea Dworkin, journalist Michelle Goldberg pointed out, "The renewed interest in Dworkin is a sign that for many women, our libidinous culture feels neither pleasurable nor liberating." "Me and my peers, we believed in this sort of fairy tale," art critic Johanna Fateman told Goldberg. "We knew where the line was, and everything on the side of consent was great, and it was an expression of our freedom. But that's not the experience of sex that a lot of people are having."

Our society may be more sexually liberated than ever before, but many men and women aren't as happy with the new status quo as the broader culture would have you believe. Yet at the same time, today's dating culture actively disdains any intensity of feeling or attachment to a certain outcome, so that we feel bad for feeling bad—and also feel like there's no room to protest. So we aim lower and ask for less, assuming that it's the best we will get.

Still, the dissatisfaction shows up in the stories women tell each other—through literature, at parties, over whisper networks, and on "shitty men" lists. The stories often go viral because they align with the ones many women haven't felt free to tell—still don't feel free to tell, because any critique of sexual permissiveness is seen as puritanical or even childish: a rejection of the loud, proud, unapologetically libertine culture that has reclaimed the word *slut* and equates promiscuity with empowerment.

Sure, the double standard around sex is shrinking, but in many of the situations we've held up as enlightened—the casual, the kinky, the polyamorous and "experimental"—the actual practice of sex seems less pleasant than it did before, when there was at least a little held back.

Rather than expanding our happiness, liberation seems to have shrunk it. We're not giddy with enjoyment or drunk on pleasure. We're Gayathri, trying to figure out how to deal with loneliness after a string of disappointments; or Nora, swearing off the opposite sex; or David, scared to even try to ask someone out.

Plus, our own confusion about what we are allowed to ask for versus what we actually seek, and what we end up getting when we play it as cool as we're supposed to, contributes to a pain all its own.

It's hard to admit that this could be the case, because it then implies that improvement might necessitate a narrowing of our options, *less* ability to maximize choice. So we double down.

Everything would be better, this pushback goes, if there were even *fewer* constraints, if women really *could* do anything, as we were promised would happen as society progressed. The real problem with sex today, we tell ourselves, is that we don't yet have perfect parity, that we still don't have full access to all our options. We haven't fully realized our modern values of privacy and autonomy. We haven't quite managed to be totally self-contained. The way that we have sex still, somehow, manages to have unpredictable—and unwanted—effects on people outside of ourselves. And those people in turn have a power over our own experience that we never agreed to give them.

With the problem reframed as one of constraint, it seems like there's a conveniently simple solution: to achieve the ideal sexual world that we desire, we just need to realize freedom more completely. By freedom we mean more privacy, more space, less connection, and less constraint.

Oddly, though, this solution always seems just over the horizon, just a little way out. For all of our striving over decades and even centuries of protest, we still haven't reached it.

This could be because total success is always an illusion. Perfect freedom is our utopian image, and those are—by their very nature—impossible to achieve. Utopia, after all, means "no place." You can't get there. It would mean the end of history, the end of striving, and humans are always in motion.

But it could also be because our ideal solution is wrong. Maybe perfect freedom isn't the answer at all.

In fact, what we need for better sex might be *more* connectedness, more interdependence, a greater acceptance of the realities of our contingent existence. The best sexual world is perhaps a *less* free one. After all, we've been moving in the direction of ever more sexual liberation, and it clearly hasn't served us as well as we might have thought.

What We Wanted Versus What We Got

The original feminist movements did advocate for more freedom: specifically, for women to have the social, economic, political, and personal freedom that would allow them to make their own choices about their lives, rather than have their experience be defined by or dictated to them by men.

But the understanding of what this freedom might look like shifted over time. For first-wave American feminists in the late nineteenth century, the extension of voting rights to white women was seen as the clearest goal. But by the end of the 1960s, radical feminists were calling for a full reorientation of society: eliminating male privilege and thereby ending the subjugation of women. Gender equality was a means of giving women the freedom to live their lives to the fullest.

The invention and mainstreaming of the contraceptive pill was seen as the practical key to women's emancipation from the tyranny of biology. But women's self-actualization was the psychological key that would unlock any larger shift. Rather than regarding their bodies with skepticism and their desires as unimportant, women were invited to embrace themselves—all of themselves, including their sexuality—as part of the movement toward gender parity. "The larger reimagining of sexual pleasure as a crucial part of life—one worth fighting for and talking about—and the sense that sexual freedom was ultimately *political*, were shared tenets of both the women's movement and the sexual revolution," wrote journalist Ariel Levy.

The midcentury feminist vision of sexual revolution was still a utopian one: of equality between men and women, allowing both the freedom to experience a life more fully human. Success here would depend on a cultural and personal revolution in which both genders were equally valued. True freedom would demand equal sharing of power, resources, and respect. And sexuality, Germaine Greer wrote in 1970, "must be rescued from the traffic between powerful and powerless, masterful and mastered . . . to become a form of communication between potent, gentle, tender people."

This total transformation of society would be a heavy and disruptive shift. But a different conversation about what freedom looked like was happening at the same time. It would take advantage of women's newfound ability to have unconstrained sex, but leave the more intractable questions of parity, value, and the ultimate aims of "revolution" by the wayside.

IN 1953 HUGH HEFNER founded *Playboy* magazine as both a model and an instruction manual for the modern bachelor. It was a celebration of consumption and a paean to libertinism. The introduction to the magazine's first issue famously extolled the virtues of the bachelor pad, where a savvy young man might be found "mixing up cocktails and an hors d'oeuvre or two, putting a little mood music on the phonograph and inviting in a female acquaintance for a quiet discussion of Picasso, Nietzsche, jazz, sex."

The sex part was essential. According to the "Playboy philosophy," a series of musings and propositions published monthly by its editor in chief, casual sex—previously frowned upon by polite society—was normal. Actually, it was more than normal; it was a crucial aspect of the good life. And now that women were freed up by readily available contraception (and a cursory understanding of feminist arguments for sexual expression), the playmate's role was to giggle and play along.

This new vision of sexuality didn't promote any meaningful sort of gender equality. The ideal woman was still seen as nondemanding and compliant; the only real difference was that she was now eager to have uncommitted sex. Still, *Playboy* billed itself as a symbol of freedom for everyone, and Hefner thought of himself not as a creep (which he was) but as a radical and even a feminist. "My naked girls," Hefner later said, were "a symbol of disobedience, a triumph of sexuality, an end of Puritanism."

Of course, it wasn't just men who were defining freedom and success on those terms. Copywriter Helen Gurley Brown published the bestselling book *Sex and the Single Girl* in 1962, selling two million copies in three weeks and going on to become the editor in chief of *Cosmopolitan* magazine.

Brown was Hefner's female equivalent, a rollicking urban adventurist in the newly liberated 1960s, determined to make the single woman—like the bachelor—the "glamour girl of our times." Her book and magazine were instruction manuals to personal, financial, and especially sexual independence.

Again, sex was essential, but so was economics. *Sex and the Single Girl* was originally conceived as a guidebook for the self-made, sexual, and extremely ambitious single woman about town; it was as much advice about how to thrive in the new world of pink-collar jobs as it was advice about how to have an amusing affair with a married man. Brown's advice centered around how a young single woman could use her sexuality to achieve career success and individual happiness. Social equity wasn't the goal; economic advancement was. "Get to a man by dealing with him on his professional level," she wrote. "Then stay around to charm and sexually zonk him."

Machiavellian, maybe. Still, underlying Brown's thinking was the radical-for-its-time proposition, shared by second-wave feminists, that sexual pleasure and fulfillment were both important and acceptable for women to desire. (Brown herself identified as a "devout feminist.") But in her advertising-trained hands, it often read as though the ability to have copious, unabashed sex was the *most* important kind of freedom that a modern woman could have, and that being seen as equal in dignity to one's male counterparts mattered less than being able to live an equally sex- and consumption-filled life.

Her philosophy suggested that gendered social inequality was immutable, that sex was basically the only form of power available to women, and thus that for women, sex's best use was not as a means to affection, connection, or self-discovery, but as a means to work the system. Rather than upending the patriarchy, the goal was to play well within it. Real freedom came from being at the top of your game.

FOR A GOOD NUMBER of second-wave feminists, the glow of the sexual revolution began to wear off even before the sixties came to a close. As the *Playboy* and *Cosmo*-girl modes of "freedom" began to outstrip the ideals of radical equality and shared dignity that the movement had originally championed, it became obvious that for all the talk of liberating women by equalizing opportunities for sexual pleasure, men seemed like the biggest beneficiaries.

Utopia is hard. Hard to explain, hard to actualize, and hard to sell. For women to have sex on equal terms with men, we really *would* have to tear down a whole system based on women's subordination. But misogyny and the patriarchy hadn't gone away with the invention of the National Organization for Women. And in a society that had increasingly adopted individualism as its organizing principle and more money as its highest goal, high-minded aspirations of equality and human dignity didn't stand much of a chance.

It's not surprising that the radical feminists of the 1960s didn't immediately succeed in bringing their idealistic vision to full fruition. What was surprising was the speed and the efficiency with which their ideas were co-opted. Feminism was repackaged as calling for a different vision of female freedom—one that was less about realizing one's full potential within society than about freeing oneself from societal responsibilities: empowerment, capitalist style.

THE #GIRLBOSS FEMINISM of the 2010s was this approach on steroids. Coined by Nasty Gal founder Sophia Amoruso, the term signified a feminism in which even sex took a back seat to economic success, and economic success came not by changing the system but by swapping in a woman for the man at the top of the corporate ladder and making her accountable to no one but herself.

The way in which female advancement was construed in popular culture had parted ways completely with the cutting-edge utopian conversations of the feminist movement. Success was now defined by the ability of women to claim the economic and social power that had formerly been dominated by men, which would ostensibly allow them to act with as little regard for others as powerful men did. And sex became less an avenue of liberation than another exhausting venue in which to perform that achievement.

"Capitalist society," in the words of critic Sophie Lewis, "is centrally predicated on commanding us all, women especially, to unrepress ourselves, to talk about sex constantly as though 'confessing' something innate, and, always and ever, to enjoy!" This positivity was both a virtue and an imperative, one that women especially had earned and ought to put to use. But the effect was less pleasurable than oppressive. To succeed in this society, you have to be hot, thin, rich, *and* be loudly and proudly having great (and appropriately boundary-pushing) sex.

At a certain point, connection, community, real enjoyment— those the culture could take or leave. The grand plan of smashing a patriarchal system that centered male preferences and pleasure had morphed into the modest goal of simply being able to claim power within it, and maximal independence was crucial to that goal.

It's commonly understood that in order to succeed in an increasingly competitive economy, you need the freedom to put yourself first. What's valued is not the ability to fully express yourself or connect in new ways. Rather, the goal is complete economic flexibility and room for total market optimization: no ties, no emotions, nothing that would keep you from positioning yourself to best compete in the open market.

Journalist Hanna Rosin's 2012 article "Boys on the Side" provided the quintessential snapshot of the sexual revolution's final evolution, celebrating college hookup culture as the key to feminist progress and eventual equality. Progress was defined, of course, as unlimited potential for an individual's career advancement and thus financial reward, to finally pull even with or maybe even surpass the opposite sex in the race to the economic top.

"To a surprising degree, it is women—not men—who are perpetuating [hookup] culture, especially in school, cannily manipulating it to make space for their success, always keeping their own ends in mind," she wrote. "An overly serious suitor fills the same role an accidental pregnancy did in the 19th century: a danger to be avoided at all costs, lest it get in the way of a promising future." The piece went on to describe how college girls could best optimize for sexual encounters without career interruption. "The ambitious women calculate that having a relationship would be like a four-credit class, and they don't always have time for it, so instead they opt for a lighter hookup."

This was the freedom to use sex as a means to individual pleasure, but also to sever oneself from any responsibilities or ties that might hinder you in a cutthroat capitalist system—a vision much more reminiscent of Helen Gurley Brown than of care feminists like Audre Lorde. The new theory was that by treating sex as callously and distantly as it seemed that men always had, women could wield their power. And rather than reaching for a radical vision of human dignity and connection within a new social model of gender equality, this interpretation of the female revolution encouraged women to settle for a baseline parity within the toxic norm.

The new feminism of the 1990s and 2000s was simply to

embrace whatever the patriarchy had already deemed valuable—sex on demand, lack of emotion, a quick climb up the economic ladder—and then make it the property of women instead of just men. The best expression of women's freedom was the ability to make sex objects out of others and reap the material benefits. Dependency was pathologized as weakness, and connection was seen as a risk.

Resetting the Terms

In 1972, feminist scholar Jo Freeman argued that when groups operate on vague and structureless terms, that structurelessness "becomes a smokescreen for the strong or the lucky to establish unquestioned hegemony over others." At the time, she was writing about competing groups within the feminist movement—but her thinking applied just as well to the broader changes in our approach to sex that have taken place since.

In the end, the sexual revolution did upend many of the rules that had previously structured society's cross-gender interactions. For women, who have always been more tightly bound by social mores, contraception and counterculture held out the promise of greater agency, a sense of sexual possibility, a broader vocabulary to express their desires, and a leveling of the playing field between men and women.

But while many things did change as the revolution progressed, some things didn't. And now that the revolution is (mostly) over, men still retain more power—politically, socially, and economically—than women. And thus it was men who established "unquestioned hegemony" in the end. In too many cases, they still seem to set the terms.

In the same essay in which she wondered whether liberation was truly possible, Ellen Willis wrote that "[sexual revolution] propaganda has undermined our main defense against [men], which was to insist, as a prerequisite to sex, that men love us or accept responsibility for us—or at least hang around long enough so that we can know what we're getting into. Now that all this is unhip we are under pressure to sleep with men on their terms, because if we won't, other women will." She continued: "Many women just give up, let men treat them like shit, and call it freedom or innate feminine altruism. A few decide that men aren't worth the hassle. But most of us try to hang in there."

Women went from pushing a radical reshaping of society to "hanging in there" in a few short years; from freedom from male domination to pressure to acquiesce to men's terms. The revolutionary ideas of the original feminists were co-opted by a dominant culture that neutralized what was radical about them and reproduced an updated version of what had already existed instead. The sexual revolution was warped by capitalism and hobbled by the strictures of misogyny and patriarchy that had remained in place.

And in chasing a particular, twisted understanding of sexual freedom within those constraints, we've defined our goals down. What we strive for as "freedom" is the freedom to be people open to anything except connection: consenting and uncomplaining. We've been empowered to be lascivious but un-caring, paying lip service to pleasure but more interested in "ex-perience." Equality between women and men now looks like equal opportunity for women to be equal to the worst sort of man—cavalier about sex and disdainful of real feeling.

CHAPTER 3

We Want to Catch Feelings

In 1973, near the height of the sexual revolution, Erica Jong published *Fear of Flying*. The novel chronicled the exploits of one Isadora Wing, a young poet seeking self-discovery and sensuality during her husband's business trip to Vienna. It was the rare bildungsroman that focused on a woman, rather than a man, struggling to define what she wanted out of life, and it hit the literary scene like a lightning bolt: Jong's debut novel was hailed as a pathbreaking work of female self-expression. Today it is read both as a feminist text and as a prototype for the *Eat, Pray, Love* genre. But what most now remember from the novel is the indelible image of the "zipless fuck."

The zipless fuck is absolutely pure. It is free of ulterior motives. There is no power game. The man is not "taking" and the woman is not "giving." No one is attempting to cuckold a husband or humiliate a wife. No one is trying to prove anything or get anything out of anyone. The zipless fuck is the purest thing there is. And it is rarer than the unicorn.

Despite that last line—"rarer than the unicorn"—the no-strings-attached sex of the zipless fuck is still held up as a cross-generational aspiration.

"I DO WONDER, like, if I know that I'm not gonna have something with the person . . . I know I'm not going to be in a relationship with them . . . like, why do I still feel the need to sleep with them?"

On a rainy December afternoon, Kris and I had met for lunch, sneaking out of both our offices for the promise of build-your-own salad at one of DC's ubiquitous young-professional lunch joints. Cheerful and outgoing, Kris was someone you would introduce your younger siblings to, knowing that she would take them under her wing. She twisted and retwisted her brunette curls as she talked, which she seemed to do at double the normal speed.

"The worst sex I've ever had was when it was a super quick thing, like last-minute thing and, like, there wasn't much of a buildup and there wasn't even, like, a big stick-around. That sucked."

She told me a story that I heard repeated over and over again by women of all ages—that they were having sex not because they really wanted to or really enjoyed it but because they felt they should. Mastering attachment-free sex was necessary in order to be liberated and urbane, to experience the truest form of pleasure and to solidify their detachment—and also to have something to tell their friends (and themselves) about what they did while they were young.

I asked her for an example.

"So here's a thing. There was this guy, I knew him through friends, and I was really into him, and I knew he was going to be moving out of the country in two weeks, and I was going on a trip to Egypt two weeks later. And so, literally, we were going to have only one night. And I knew it. So we got drinks. And I thought, like, there's some elements of intrigue here, and there's a good story to tell—first of all, he was *moving*, you know? And so I think I was into it in the moment and, like, you know, sex is great and everything." She turned wistful. "But then afterward I was like, 'It probably would have been a lot, like, easier if I hadn't.' You know what I mean? I don't think that that was necessarily a great move."

After a pause, Kris regathered her earlier brio. "It's not like I was in *love* with him. It's not like I was *heartbroken*. But it's a challenge for me sometimes the way that, you know, I feel like I should just be living in the moment. I mean, it was really great.

And who knows if our paths will cross again someday. But like, I don't know if it was really best for my emotions."

"Casual sex . . . ," she mused, thoughtfully picking over her salad, "Do I really want this? Do I really enjoy this? Or is it because I think this is what I should be doing in my twenties, what people expect of me? How much of this is for the story?"

IT MAY WELL be possible to have an Isadora Wing experience—sex existing outside of time, space, and expectations, utterly detached from the reality of life on the ground. But for most people, that is not what sex is, or how it's experienced in our day-to-day lives of flirting, dating, and hooking up.

We have sex in the context of our gender and age, our location and economic status, our insecurities and unspoken longings. And to strive for that zipless detachment, or even to assume that it is an achievable goal, confuses a cultural fiction with truth and substitutes an implausible fantasy for the reality of what most of us actually desire.

Because *is* that what we really desire? It was a curious thing, interviewing people about what they wanted from sex. Again and again, they would mention intimacy, emotion, closeness, being seen. But then they would follow up with a disclaimer, as if afraid they had misstepped and outed themselves as the repressed, swoony virgins none of us are supposed to be. "Of course, that's just my opinion! There are *plenty* of people who have truly casual sex and don't think about it at all!"

"Do you know any of those people?" I ask. Usually, the answer is no.

THE LATE 1990s and mid-aughts (not coincidentally, the years in which the average millennial was either approaching, experiencing, or just leaving their formative adolescence) were the years in which Jenna Jameson's *How to Make Love Like a Porn Star* spent weeks on bestseller lists, Kim Kardashian's leaked sex tape catapulted her to riches and fame, and *Sex and the City*, HBO's landmark series in which four single women in New York City use sex and shopping as stand-ins for personal growth, and ruin Magnolia Bakery cupcakes for everyone, was called "one of the biggest feminist movements in entertainment."

HBO's raunchy roman à clef launched a thousand dubious narratives, but most of all embodied something of a grand unified theory of all the new ways of looking at sex. The exploits of Carrie, Samantha, Miranda, and Charlotte (that I can still easily name the four main characters despite the show having gone off the air in 2004 underlines how culturally pervasive it still is) are perhaps the clearest example of a script that has since been taken up and reinforced by any number of other cultural products, and that has infiltrated the general consciousness of those who grew up in its heyday. It's a script that says that to be an adult is to be in constant collection of a variety of experiences—especially sexual ones—and that doing so is necessary in order to be mature, self-actualized, and *normal*. At the same time, you need to be "chill" about it—detached, nonchalant, not thinking too much—because the acts themselves mean very little. Sex can easily be just physical, and probably should be, in order to allow yourself the freedom to experience more, different things. It's a paradox: *having* sex matters; the sex itself does not. You're collecting encounters to make yourself ready for some final stage. But finality itself is unwanted.

"You are not supposed to say you had unfulfilling sexual experiences because you tragically wanted a boyfriend," one article in *New York* magazine's blog *The Cut* laughingly—but accurately—informs the reader: "My experiences were often negative and rueful, and so my promiscuity seems in hindsight to have been a means to some elusive end. I craved stimulus. . . . Maybe what I wanted was feeling, full stop."

According to this script, intimate encounters are acquired like so many pairs of Carrie's Manolo Blahnik shoes—and used like them, as signaling mechanisms to show that you're sophisticated and cool. And the only important actor here is you—your desires, your "personal growth," take precedence over the needs and feelings of your partner, or of any larger community. The need to secure your own status pushes encounters toward hookups rather than anything that could become entangling. And still, despite the emotional distance, the pain of breakups, the tedious sex, and the STD scares, everything will turn out just as you want—into marriage, a still-swinging single life, whatever kind of relationship you *really* desire—in the end. Carrie and Big do eventually get married—after six seasons, dozens of partners, ninety-something episodes, and a feature film allowed her to wring all possible experiences—sexual and otherwise—out of her idealized life.

BUT THE PUBLIC CONVERSATION about sex is one thing. What people really want is often another.

In 2018, *Radiolab*, a podcast from radio station WNYC, aired a three-part series called "In the No," a first-person exploration of one woman's struggle to navigate sex and communicate about consent. In the first few minutes of the first episode—an upbeat burble that suddenly takes a turn for the serious—radio maker Kaitlin Prest explains how she found herself asking those questions.

"I'm in my twenties. I left my tiny little town for the big city. I live in NYC now. I make an artsy, feminist sex radio show. Third-wave, sex-positive feminism tells me that I was onto something back in my teens. Adopting the same ruthless sexual posturing that boys are encouraged to would allow me to wield some of their power. If we fucked without feelings, we too could be free. Having slut pride would subvert the double standard, and it would force the world to recognize that women's sexual pleasure is real."

A pause.

"The only problem is that I hate casual sex."

A year or so after her *Radiolab* debut, Kaitlin and I talk on the phone. Her voice is faster-paced than it is in her radio work; she's bubbling over with opinions and stories that she shares with the confidence of your most gregarious friend. "I think that sex should be something that's about a shared, like, spiritual, emotional, psychological, and physical intimacy. That it should be something that isn't negating the person who they are."

She continues: "You know that idea of 'fuck without feelings,' that idea of slut pride? To me, I do disagree with that. I do think it's fucked up. I *don't* think that that is going down the path of trying to create a healthier world. I think we're just copying something that is demeaning and dehumanizing, which is to take someone's body and not their soul. I don't agree with that. I think that the body and the soul are connected."

When she first released her radio show, Kaitlin tells me, "the responses we got were tons and tons of women writing being like, 'Oh my God, I felt so alone, and I feel the same way.'"

OF COURSE, THE ADMONITION "not to care" is nothing new. In Jane Austen's *Pride and Prejudice*, Lizzie Bennet has to sail past an insulting Mr. Darcy with an insouciant remark to disguise her hurt. She's admonished not to let her pain show and not to let on that he (or his opinion) has any effect on her at all.

But the understanding underlying her interaction is different. In Regency England, it's obvious and acknowledged that sex, love, and romance are serious and have the power to ruin, elevate, or otherwise change the circumstances of one's life.

In the modern era, we refuse to see sex and relationships as holding that much importance. In fact, we're glad they don't. And yet it doesn't take us long to figure out that having lots of sex without consequences doesn't mean we're sexually satisfied, and that even being sexually satisfied doesn't mean we're actually fulfilled.

I spoke to therapist and bestselling author Lori Gottlieb about some of these contradictions. Based in Los Angeles, she has many clients in their twenties and thirties who are and struggling to reconcile the scripts they have absorbed with the feelings they actually have.

"I think it's a fallacy of feminism that somehow it's liberating not to care," Gottlieb told me in the course of our conversation. "If anything, that lowers your power. People think, 'I'm so empowered because I don't care. I don't care what he does or who I sleep with. I don't care!' But then you become valueless. You're saying, 'I don't care. I don't have any worth [in this encounter]. I'm not placing worth on myself.'

"There's a lot of pressure for people to act like it's not a big deal, or for them to tell themselves that it's not," she said. "It's really hard for young people to say, 'I want a relationship. I want that.'"

The Balance

There's usually a reason why we downplay our goals. It's often because we don't think that they are achievable, or because we don't want to sign ourselves up for the struggle. When it comes to sex, our desire is often strong and unruly enough that we would rather indulge it without complication, without grappling with what it might mean. Intimacy makes claims on us, after all. Embodiment is, in a real way, a trap—we can't ex-change our bodies for other ones; we can't leave ourselves. A transcendent experience might leave a mark. We might be mak-ing light of sex *because* we sense that it matters.

If sex is solely about the performance of the physical act, you can practice at it, get better, and even if you have a one-off flubbed encounter, it's not so bad. You can find better partners to do it with if one doesn't work out; you can keep on searching and learning new tricks until you find your groove. But if sex is about something larger—care, connectedness, the human expe-rience writ large—not getting it right might mean that there's something wrong with *you*. If we admit that all these things are possible, we are responsible for them. In the end being bad at "having sex" is much less frightening than being bad at being a person.

But if the extreme pleasures and risks of sex are real, even if they exist only in some of our encounters, we should be taking sex seriously—or at least more seriously than we do now.

Sex is just an act, yes, but it's one with more meaning than we give it credit for. It's an act that touches something deep and intrinsic in the human person, with the potential, at least, for the creation of something greater than the individuals involved—up to and including another human being conceived between them.

I think that many of us want something more from sex than what we have been willing to acknowledge: pleasure, yes, but also closeness, mutuality, even a sense of the sacred. It's also likely that we have been asking too much from it: self-definition, self-actualization, total fulfillment.

A new balance needs to be struck. How do we accord sex a privileged position in our lives without either putting it on a pedestal as the ultimate expression of agency—a personal achievement, a level unlocked—or walling it off as something purely holy and ineffable?

IN THE END, says Gottlieb, "I think people are really lonely. I think most people really want a partner—ultimately they want their person, they want to love and be loved. They want connection, they want the stability of that. I mean, I think that's just very human nature. We all want to love and be loved."

Across a wide span of interviews, her words seemed to echo. "I feel like being with someone in a serious way would be potentially a major contributor to increase happiness, contentment, and fulfillment," one man told me, "because you have a partner who is there for you, believes in you, who shares your fears and hopes and all that stuff. And you learn to be less selfish and you're sharing a life, you're building a life with someone. I feel like that." He summed it up: "Love sounds like a very constructive thing. I think we all want to be less alone."

More and more, we are drawn to the conclusion that sex without love—at least of some kind—leads to disappointment and disillusionment. And the flip side of this conclusion, of course, is that sex, done right, is an expression and a vehicle for something beyond "the experience": it's closeness, relationship, union with another human being. Everyone wants love of some kind, but no one wants to admit it. Maybe this is because to admit that we want such a connection is to burden ourselves with responsibilities, to ourselves and others.

One of the pleasures of sex is the sharing of the dirty little secrets about ourselves, sometimes literally. Sex is a powerful mode of bonding, especially in an unprecedentedly disconnected time. It can start a relationship or feel like the ratification of one.

"There's an element of, like . . . an intimacy that comes with it, and when you are single and sometimes lonely and, you know, seeking affection or just, like, the human touch," one woman told me, "I think there's something more to it than just the actions."

BUT IN MODERN DATING CULTURE, the ideal personality is free of responsibility and absent any strong emotions that could get in the way of self-creation or peak optimization.

"I'm told I don't have to try to justify love, which contains at least a small percentage of unsolvable mystery, but I just can't stand the thought of seeming irrationally carried away by emotion," says the female narrator in Lauren Oyler's zeitgeisty novel *Fake Accounts*, as she downplays the stirrings of a genuine crush after a sexual encounter. "I believe it hurts the feminist cause. And worse, it makes me personally look bad."

This studied irony embodies what writer Alana Massey memorably described as the tyranny of chill:

Chill has now slithered into our romantic lives and forced those among us who would like to exchange feelings and accountability to compete in the Blasé Olympics with whomever we are dating. . . . Chill asks us to remove the language of courtship and desire lest we appear invested somehow in other human beings. It is a game of chicken where the first person to confess their frustration or confusion loses. Chill is a sinister refashioning of "Calm down!" from an enraging and highly gendered command into an admirable attitude. Chill presides over the funeral of reasonable expectations. Chill takes and never gives. Chill is pathologically unfeeling but not even interesting enough to kill anyone.

How fun.

We aren't invited to bring our whole selves to the table, even though for many of us our greatest wish from sex is to be seen; instead, we're urged to set aside anything that might stick in the gears of the market—the weight of attachment, the drag of scruples, the friction of care.

THE THING IS, no one really wants this much chill. This kind of "freedom" wasn't the original goal of the sexual revolution, and it certainly can't be described as a success. "After throwing ourselves into a life of never being beholden to nor invested in nor emotionally vulnerable with the person we were shtupping," blogger Charlotte Shane wrote, "we realized the warnings were true: complete freedom looked and felt a lot like loneliness."

We can now fuck without feelings, but let's be honest—the

feelings were the fun part. Most of us were never just in it for the five to thirty minutes of physical pleasure. The reality is that the dispassionate, disconnected, empty approach to sexuality was never what we wanted, and is barely even possible: engaging in intimate acts begets feelings, it's *natural*. Total freedom was never a realistic goal, and the warped vision of freedom we celebrate now fails to satisfy. And our confusion about what we're allowed to ask for versus what we actually want, and the distance between what we want and what we end up getting when we play it as cool as we're supposed to, can add up to a particularly bitter discontent.

WE VALUE SEX because of its intimacy—however that is defined. We seek it out because it can be a unique place of private connection. But at the same time, that connection makes sex particularly fraught. People can hurt each other.

Yet the solution isn't to perfect our "chill," to avoid emotion and become the most hard-hearted versions of ourselves.* It's to embrace the risk and, with attention and care, mitigate it where we can. While being radically individualistic might protect me better from certain forms of domination and leave me free to optimize in many directions (success in the market, it's worth

---

* In fact, early feminists warned against this. "The [1984] Nightmare is directly the product of the attempt to imagine a society in which women have become like men, crippled in the identical way, thus destroying a delicate balance of interlocking dependencies," wrote Shulamith Firestone in 1970.

noting, is never guaranteed), this sort of freedom does not necessarily better equip me to meet the most meaningful challenges that we encounter in human life.

"Freedom," in isolation, is not an actual good. It can be a frame that allows us space to seek the good within it, but it's not the good itself. Freedom doesn't protect us from loneliness, from a lack of affection, from the failure to connect with others in our world. Because this connection, rather than economic success, momentary physical pleasure, or even ego gratification, is what we as humans crave most deeply. We may want liberation today, but we want meaning tomorrow, and for the rest of our lives.

The problem with the "zipless fuck" is not that it's too difficult to achieve. The problem is that it's a fantasy, and one that distracts us from the truth of what we really desire. By idealizing an illusion, we ignore the realities that would actually help us flourish. But to understand this inevitably raises the question: What other realities are we ignoring?

CHAPTER 4

Men and Women Are Not the Same

"IDEA: I WANT TO WRITE an invoice to my exes for my egg freezing costs." On a sultry Wednesday afternoon in August, my phone pinged with this text from Laura, one of my closest female friends. After years of sex, dating, and relationships—obviously, consented to at the time—she had come to the realization that she had not been as well-informed, or as justly treated, as she thought. Her latest long-term relationship had just ended due to her boyfriend's unwillingness to commit. Now she was thirty-three and about to embark on the expensive process of freezing her eggs. Or she had been, until the fertility clinics had all closed under the pandemic shutdown, just after she had gotten test results that starkly detailed her "depleted ovarian reserve." Her time had been wasted, and the clock was still ticking. Reparations were due.

Laura was joking—the sort of nihilistic humor we had all resorted to by that point in the pandemic—but I felt her pain. At the time, I was in a relationship myself. While it seemed like it might be the one, it also might *not* be; I just wasn't sure, and six months of lockdown hadn't helped. And yet I was in my thirties, and I knew that if we were to break up, I would be that much further from having a chance to have the family I had always hoped for. My own supply of eggs would continue to dwindle in the time that it would take to meet someone new, and there wouldn't be much that I could do about it—especially in the midst of a pandemic that made dating seem even more like Russian roulette than usual.

I *also* knew that my boyfriend wouldn't have these worries, since male fertility exists under far fewer constraints. Men seem to have it easier in this regard—something I had always known in the back of my mind, but that was now coming to the forefront in a way that I very much did not appreciate.

TODAY THE MAINSTREAM VIEW sees men and women as broadly similar, sexually speaking, differing only in that women have had to put up with more patriarchal oppression from society. And in the service of closing that final divide, we have gone from "Men and women should both be allowed to explore their sexuality" to pretending that sex isn't a unique kind of physical interaction, one that might affect men and women differently.

But indeed it is, and it does. And casual sex, in particular, disadvantages women.

Sex, Gender, and Equality

We are taught to assume that everyone is equal and that—minor exceptions aside—each party comes to an encounter from a similar place of freedom, constrained only by our wills. Women and men are basically interchangeable and approach sex, love, and desire in the same way (or ought to, anyway). Any broader difference should be ascribed to cultural conditioning or individual choice; nothing is inherent in biology.

The problem is that this isn't true. As our own experiences make clear, our biologies and our biographies come with us into the bedroom. The structures that otherwise shape our lives don't cease to exist once we start having sex. Women remain women, with all of the physical characteristics, structural constraints, and social programming that come with our gender. And men remain men.

It's not hard to understand why we embraced this particular fiction of equivalence so easily. We learned in high school civics that the social contract we make with government and society, and the various social contracts we place beneath it, are happy exercises of freedom on a level playing field. A set of individuals with equal rights and equal capabilities make free choices about how they organize their lives, exchanging this right or that privilege for this access or that good. They do so in full understanding of what that trade means, and with full opportunity to agree or back out. We cannot and should not criticize these individual choices—they are valid because the people who made them say that they are. We create our own worlds.

Meanwhile, for the majority of the past century, feminists have fought and are still fighting for women to be seen as individuals, as adults, as worthy of participation in the social contract despite centuries of history in which female biology was seen as a reason for female subordination. Only recently has society begun to regularly acknowledge women's agency, sexual and otherwise, and see women as equals to men. These victories are not yet secure, and it feels risky to jeopardize the fragile acceptance of women's equality by focusing too hard on where differences between men and women might still lie.

The ethic of consent, as it's understood today, draws upon our allegiance to both understandings. Women must be seen as individuals, equal agents. And as long as two individuals have both freely agreed to something, we are content to assume that no more discussion need be had.

This conclusion comes as a particular relief when we're forced to think about sex, the topic that everyone has simultaneously agreed is essential to address but remains wildly uncomfortable to discuss and horribly fraught to cast judgment upon. If two parties have consented to do something with each other, we can lower the curtain on their activities and leave them to it without having to worry about whether one party or the other is being taken advantage of, or what—if any—repercussions their activities might have on anyone else or on society at large.

But the qualifiers we add around consent in practice suggest that reality often fails to line up with our ethical ideal. Bodily inequality is real. We don't exist independently of each other, floating in the void, with equal abilities, equal resources, and equally respected rights. And because of that, even in situations that have been mutually consented to, things are rarely even.

Unfortunately, that remains especially true for women. While we can and do make our own choices when it comes to sex—about what to consent to and what to reject, what our preferences are and how we want to express them—our choices are often more constrained than men's, in ways both visible and invisible. Women are still the more vulnerable party when it comes to sex.

In the United States, the FDA approved the oral contraceptive pill for women in 1960, allowing women to sever sex from the inevitability of childbearing. "Modern woman is at last free as a man is free to dispose of her own body," wrote journalist Clare Boothe Luce. The Equal Pay Act, passed in 1963, and Title IX, passed in 1972, outlawed discrimination in pay and access to educational programming (including sports) on the basis of sex.

The push to minimize sex difference was both practical and cultural. In 1990, philosopher Judith Butler published the landmark *Gender Trouble*, in which she argued that gender was a performance and identity was mutable. In later work, she further developed the idea: sex was not "a bodily given on which the construct of gender is artificially imposed, but . . . a *cultural* norm which governs the materialization of bodies." Popular culture quickly took up that ideal. In Gatorade's iconic "Anything you can do I can do better" commercial in 1999, Mia Hamm squared off successfully against Michael Jordan. At a certain point, the psychologist Steven Pinker suggests, "the belief that men and women are psychologically indistinguishable became sacred"; questioning that belief in public was taboo.

WHILE THE TWENTY-FIRST CENTURY may have advanced social equity, it didn't do away with biology. Cisgender men and women—who make up most of the population*—are differentiated by chromosomes, hormones, and anatomy.

Men, on average, are 15 to 20 percent larger than women, with more muscle mass and significantly greater physical strength. The majority of men could likely kill a woman with their bare hands. Hence the mental calculus that women face whenever they want to reject a man's sexual advances: Will he hurt me?

And even though gender is to some extent a construct à la Judith Butler, it still shapes the way we experience the world—in our solicitude (or lack thereof) for one another, in our comfort with lodging complaint, and in the expectations we hold for our lives. For all our interventions, biological inequality still tilts the playing field.

---

* Intersex people are estimated to make up from 0.02 to 1.7 percent of the population, depending on definition, and between 0.3 to 0.6 percent of Americans identify as nonbinary or gender-nonconforming. Approximately 0.6 percent of adults identify as transgender. In this chapter, generalizations about the sexes refer primarily to cisgender men and women.

Pregnancy

My social milieu is educated, young, forward-thinking; the swinging singles of Helen Gurley Brown's wildest dreams. None of my girlfriends are hoping for a surprise pregnancy, none of my male friends are looking to become a father as the result of a one-night stand. Zero people of either sex want an STI. But for all our carefree posturing when it comes to hookups, we still do understand that sex comes with some risk. And women, even when they have consented to sex, end up bearing more of it.

"The one time we had sex without protection," one friend, a thirty-three-year-old tech worker, revealed, "my period was late. And I *freaked out*. My boyfriend offered to pay for Plan B, which, thanks, but . . . fifty dollars is the least of my problems right now. And then he said that he would 'support me in whatever I chose to do,' which, again, thanks, but . . . it kind of made me feel like I was more on my own. But I mean, in the end I would have had to decide by myself, right? Like, it would be me who was pregnant, not him."

She did get emergency contraception, and waited it out. And she didn't end up pregnant—luckily, in her mind. "I think I would have had an abortion in the end, but I didn't *want* to. But at the same time, I couldn't imagine having a baby. I mean, I'm still scared of the idea of pregnancy, honestly. And my parents would lose it, and my job is insane, and I . . . I just have other things that I wanted to do. I feel like my life would have had to stop."

Most of the women I know went on birth control early, and

have stayed on. Men, meanwhile, could just agree to use condoms or be willing to cough up the cost of emergency contraception if a situation went awry.

The game here was lopsided. If the risk of sex was an un-wanted child, women assumed the majority of the exposure even with precautions in place, and still do. Because—to state the obvious—women still do get pregnant. And men don't.

Pregnancy can be a gift, but it is also, definitely, a risk. De-spite conservative politicians' reminders that "pregnancy is not a life-threatening illness," approximately eight hundred women in the United States die every year during pregnancy or within the forty-two days after delivery, making even the prospect of pro-creation a fundamentally dangerous prospect for the female sex.

But even the healthy delivery of an unexpected child can up-end a woman's life, changing the course of her future—not to mention bringing a new human being into existence, with their own needs and future to contend with. Beyond the obvious stress of an unplanned major life event, there are significant—and some-times irreversible—changes to the body, and often setbacks in financial stability and education that compound going forward. Meanwhile, the closest thing to an enforceable, durable conse-quence for a male partner from an accidental pregnancy might be child support—of course, only about 61 percent of required child-support payments are ever made. Even if the pregnancy is followed by a durable relationship, the burden of childcare tends to fall primarily on women, often limiting their chances to pur-sue personal goals or advance in their careers. The COVID-19 pandemic exposed how enduring this split is, even in the most egalitarian-seeming partnerships. (In one groan-inducing *New York Times* survey, nearly a quarter of men claimed to be responsible for childcare during lockdown. Two percent of women agreed.)

We take it for granted that abortion and birth control have mostly mitigated these obvious inequities, setting men and woman on an equal footing, one not haunted by the specter of an unplanned baby crying as they head off to work. But while their arrival did help to delink sex from pregnancy, freeing up twenty-first-century men and women to enact their sexual desires in the short term without constantly thinking of the consequences, some parties still remain less burdened than others.

In her bestseller *Taking Charge of Your Fertility*, health educator Toni Weschler baldly states the facts: "While the pill was originally designed to sexually emancipate women, it has also had the effect of burdening the woman with the sole responsibility of birth control." There are the known side effects of the type of hormonal contraception, which most women rely on for decades at a time: weight gain, low libido, depression, anxiety, dangerous blood clots, suicidal ideation and attempts. Any woman can tell you a story—or relate her own experience—of feeling like a different person while on the pill. And yet it's assumed to be a fair trade, or at least one that women should quietly accept. (In contrast, a study of a male birth control option was killed in 2016 after men complained of side effects like . . . acne.)

The pill is 99 percent effective (under perfect use; typical use drops it down to 91 percent), but it isn't 100 percent. Neither are any of the other methods—patch, ring, shot, IUD—that women are asked to shoulder for decades on end (the most common age for beginning hormonal contraceptives is sixteen). Still, 45 percent of the six million pregnancies in the United States each year are unintended. In 2001, some 48 percent of women experiencing an unintended pregnancy had been using contraception in the month their child was conceived. And even if the pill were 100 percent effective, the semipermanent hormone disruption of the female sex is a high price for women to have to pay for entry into the professional or sexual worlds.

Abortion is often alluded to as a final bulwark for women's sexual freedom: if the risk of a pregnancy still exists, at least there is a backstop. Women don't *have* to put up with something that men don't. But ending a pregnancy is rarely a simple or consequence-free choice. In an article for the website The Everygirl, one woman describes her thought process as she waited for an abortion: "Having a child would mean having to press pause on the initial goals I had set for myself. . . . Knowing that I was about to say goodbye to the baby I wasn't going to meet, grief began to crawl into my veins." Even if the procedure itself seems simple, the psychological effects can linger.

The Clock

Worry about the asymmetry of pregnancy risk in sexual encounters is, of course, predicated on the assumption that neither the man nor the woman wants to be pregnant, at least not in the very near future. But what about the times that we might?

With that uplifting text chain about egg-freezing costs lodged firmly in my mind on a hot August afternoon, I bicycled downtown to interview Micah, a researcher in DC. Cultured and confident, he had lived across Europe and Asia before settling down (-ish) in an upscale part of the city. We sat on his roof deck two meters apart, steaming like germ-avoidant dumplings under the summer sun.

COVID, he said, had made him become more thoughtful about dating and sex. "You know, I'm in my thirties. I want to settle down, give my parents grandchildren." Rather than going back to a prepandemic lifestyle, he was trying to be more deliberate in how he went about his romantic life. Under lockdown, meeting people at work or parties was off the table, so he resorted to dating apps, which he despised. "I remember when I first came to DC I was really excited about using the apps. But now I hate it. It's like the paradox of choice." His solution to sorting through this barrage of females? "Sometimes I'll limit the age range. I think right now my more discerning age range is, like, twenty-four to thirty-four."

Micah is thirty-six.

I ask why he stops at thirty-four. I'm feeling a little stung, even though I'm (mercifully?) still within his range.

"I mean, honestly, the kids issue." He pauses, then continues: "Not that people can't have kids after thirty-four! But then think about, like, okay, we meet, we date for like eight months or something. We get engaged, then we want to spend some time just me and her before we actually have kids. So she's thirty-six when we get married, which is impossible if she's my age, because I'm about to turn thirty-seven. So she's the age I am now. She could be like thirty-six or even thirty-seven."

The math is a whirlwind.

"And then there's another two years before we probably have kids, at best. So we're talking about thirty-eight. Thirty-eight is danger—" He stops himself before he says it. "I mean, come on. That's going to present some challenges."

Not for him, though.

AFTER PASSING THE age of thirty, conversations like this one become less and less unusual, and more and more alarming. Since 1978, when *The Washington Post* introduced the term *biological clock* to the modern lexicon, women have been reminded constantly that our fertility takes a nosedive after the age of thirty-five, with egg counts declining and the risk of complications rising. The average forty-year-old woman has a 5 percent chance of getting pregnant in any given month. By age forty-five, it's 1 percent. Men experience declines too, but, as one fertility clinic gently puts it, "male fertility decline with age is less significant and less dramatic than what women experience." Mick Jagger famously fathered his eighth child at seventy-three—his girlfriend was twenty-nine at the time.

Artificial reproductive technology (ART) has aimed to level the playing field, expanding women's runway to have children on their terms. But though the technology has advanced in leaps and bounds, it's still time-consuming, emotionally draining, and expensive. And the majority of these costs, too, tend to accrue to women. Thousands of women decide to have their eggs frozen and stored as an insurance policy for the future, but the methodology is still fairly new and the process isn't cheap. *Cosmopolitan* magazine outlined an average out-of-pocket bill: $500 for an initial appointment, $5,500 for medications, $9,000 for the actual procedure, and $600 for a year of storage, for a total of $15,600 in the first year (most women store for longer than that). And when it comes time for in vitro fertilization—whether to treat infertility or to turn those frozen eggs into a baby, the cost for a single round can run up to $20,000, which usually isn't covered by insurance.

That assumes that it all works, which, of course, is not guaranteed. The success rate of egg freezing varies dramatically, and many women never go on to use their eggs. The majority of IVF cycles end in failure. Though it has extended the window of fertility for some, technology has not eliminated reproductive inequalities between men and women—and likely never will.

Commitment

Pregnancy (or the lack thereof) is not the only factor influencing how we have sex. But even when children aren't on the table, men and women's preferences have a tendency to diverge in a way that gives men comparative power.

Micah continued to give me the rundown, at least as he understood it.

"I mean, I guess we all know, but it's hard to talk about it.

But men are different in some ways, obviously. So that plays into this. How we view sex is obviously relevant. So even when women say, like, 'Oh, they're down to just have sex' and you're explicit that, 'Hey, you're not looking for a relationship, this is going to be casual,' in my experience, there are very few women who are content with it, just staying in that arrangement if you keep on seeing them over a month or two. Almost inevitably, in my experience. Maybe there are exceptions to the rule."

Saying as much seemed to make him nervous, as though he were breaking some unspoken taboo. He twisted an abandoned wine cork into the table, gathering momentum, before going on to tell me about his experience with a past girlfriend.

"You know, we met in Singapore, and that's where we started seeing each other. Then she was in Singapore and I was in Seattle. That's not long distance, it's *super* long distance. So we agreed on an open, 'don't ask, don't tell' situation, because she was a self-styled really 'open mind' about sex and relationships. Of course, predictably—it's almost too obvious—she's like, 'I can't do this.'"

The last lines came out in a gust. "And my guess is that eighty percent of women who would think they can do open relationships are like, 'I thought I could do it. I can't.'"

THE ANECDOTE RANKLED, but it had the ring of truth—maybe because it reflected my own feelings, and those of the women I knew. For all our protestations about our flexibility and openness to experimentation, we mostly were interested in finding our one partner, hopefully for the long term. Dating definitely yielded good stories and some amount of self-knowledge, but committed, monogamous relationships tended to be the gold standard, for both sexual pleasure and emotional satisfaction. We might try for it, but emotionless sex wasn't easy.

"For [sex] to be good," Kris had told me in our lunchtime conversation, "it's gonna have to matter. Like, to some extent, you're going to want to actually feel connected to that person in the moment. And if you are, if you can reach that level, then it's not going to be easy to just move on from that—there was something there."

She spoke for many of us when she continued: "I feel like I've been in denial about that at times. I've been like, 'It's just super casual and super easy and whatever,' but . . . no. There's always something there."

A SURVEY OF **1,600** PEOPLE from fifty-two countries asked respondents whether they would like to have more than one partner per month. Twenty-five percent of heterosexual men and 29 percent of homosexual men said yes. Only 4 percent of heterosexual women and 5 percent of lesbians agreed. In a survey of more than 23,000 Americans, men were 13 percent more likely than women to say that they were interested in having an open relationship.

It's not that surprising, when one considers that women experience pleasure in different ways and to a different degree than men in sexual encounters, especially depending on the level of commitment. Studies show that women are more likely to regret casual and uncommitted sexual interactions, while men's regrets are more often about missed opportunities to have sex. When college students were asked whether they wished for "more opportunities" to hook up on their campuses, 48 percent of men said yes, compared with only 16 percent of women.

And while relationship quality affects both men's and women's sexual enjoyment, scholars have found that emotional factors tend to be particularly relevant for women's sexual response, that women tend to connect sex and love more than men, and that they achieve orgasm with regularity only after repeated encounters with the same person or, more reliably, in committed relationships. In fact, the commitment of their partner was a strong predictor of women's sexual enjoyment. Forty-two percent of college men said they'd had an orgasm in their most recent uncommitted hookup, compared with only 16 percent of women.

Why? Some of it might be social conditioning: women are taught, more than men, to feel shame over uncommitted encounters and to advocate less for their own pleasure, especially with someone they don't know well. But biology tends to play a role here, too. Men and women both have bad sex and good sex, but when sex is bad for women, it tends to be really, *really* bad. And uncommitted relationships—where partners have less incentive to build an understanding of each other's likes, dislikes, sensitivities—tend to produce more bad sex.

Research shows that women tend to experience more pain during sexual encounters than their male counterparts. A 2015 research study led by Debby Herbenick, the principal investigator of the National Survey of Sexual Health and Behavior, found that in their most recent instance of vaginal intercourse 30 percent of women reported experiencing pain, compared with 5 percent of men, and 72 percent of women report pain during anal sex, compared with only 15 percent of men. Moreover, "large proportions" of respondents don't tell their partners when sex hurts.

For men, bad sex might look like not orgasming, or maybe being a little bit bored or anxious on the way there. For women, bad sex looks like blood, tearing, actual tooth-gritting pain. The highs might be equally high, but the lows are significantly lower. There's more at stake for women in each encounter. This is something that the assumption of pure equality tends not to take into account: women may not be coequal partners at all.

"I think so often for women it's not the actual act of sex that is enjoyed so much as the buildup to it—the foreplay and the other stuff," one woman told me. "Then the sex is just like 'Okay, you sealed the deal. You gave the man what he wants.' Then you can at least have an excuse to lay there and cuddle."

Or as one college student put it, as her friends nodded along: "So many people I know are like, 'Yeah, it was fun! . . . And then we had sex.'"

It's impolitic to suggest that women may be more inclined to monogamy than men, or less sex-motivated in certain respects. Men want love and relationships too, after all, and different timelines or physiology don't necessarily lead to predation or indifference. But being more dependent on a partner's commitment level in order to experience pleasure—whether due to biological factors or social expectations shaped by gender—often leaves women more invested in relationships than men, a power imbalance that many of our pro-sex analyses tend not to take into account.

Equal Exchange?

In his *Critique of Dialectical Reason*, Jean-Paul Sartre describes a supposedly free and mutual exchange that is in reality marked by unacknowledged inequality. "It is just that one of them pretends . . . not to notice that the Other is forced by the constraint of needs to sell himself as a material object."

You don't need to go so far as to say that women are selling themselves as objects (though you might, considering the amount of self-objectification many women undergo to make themselves seem like worthy partners) to suggest that in the wilderness of dating, these mutual exchanges aren't as free, equal, or *mutual* as they pretend to be. Women tend to want children earlier in life than men, and more urgently. In survey after survey, women are found to be significantly more likely than men to say that they are seeking a committed relationship.

In many cases, to attract and keep a partner—salvaging the possibility of a future relationship, family, and children—women will consent to things that they would rather not—sex that is unpleasant or degrading or that comes with no promise of commitment attached, only the *potential* of commitment, dangling hopefully somewhere in the future.

This is a space ripe for coercion, of a kind that our current understanding of consent does not take into account. Women are more susceptible to having their time wasted by men and regretting it later. Obviously, much of this sex is consented to at the time. But simply getting consent in this context may not take into account the other person's good, what might bring them sustainable happiness in the long term. Again, a minimalist ethic suffices, but if we're looking for a better sexual culture overall, we should want more.

Because of course, these women *could*, if they really wanted to, say no. They could make the choice not to consent, a choice that—in a post-#MeToo environment—would likely be respected. They're free women having sex with free men.

But what kind of choice is really being offered? There's the freedom to say no, of course, and take what comes with it: uncertainty, loneliness, and the acutely painful feeling of your biological clock ticking away. There's also the freedom to say yes: to submit to something that you don't really want, in the hope of some possibility in the future. But the idea that one's biological vulnerability might be incorporated into the debate and made allowances for isn't really on the table.

One could say that life is full of choices, and full of outcomes that mix the bitter with the sweet. No option is perfect. And of course, that's true. The problem with the consent here is that it sublimates the complexity of these choices and the inequality inherent in the choice. There's no room to question whether the options you are given are fair and, if they aren't, what might be done to make them better. There's no acknowledgment that one party may be operating under circumstances that are more constrained, or that one person may have more to lose and should for that reason be treated with care.

There's no room to complain and little possibility of interrogating the system.

You consented to this, after all.

Intimate Justice

Sarah McClelland's voice is gentle, balanced, and slightly halting. She delivers her words slowly, as if she's turning each one over in her mind before she releases it out into the world. It reminds me that she's an academic—a professor in the Psychology and Women's and Gender Studies departments at the University of Michigan, to be precise. But it also fits the topic we're discussing, the pitfall-strewn question of how to think about sex.

"My plea in intimate justice is to *stop*," she says. "To stop thinking about everything as the same."

In 2009, Professor McClelland began to popularize the concept of intimate justice. The theory was originally meant to help guide research on sexual satisfaction—it argued that researchers who asked whether sex was "satisfactory" for participants weren't going far enough in examining whether sexual outcomes were distributed equally. In addition to asking for surface-level appraisals, McClelland thought, researchers needed to ask questions about the nature of the benchmarks being used to measure satisfaction, and the history of the groups and individuals being assessed. Scientists needed to be aware of and make adjustments for the ways in which inequality showed up in sex.

Professor McClelland continued, "This has implications for how we treat ourselves, how we treat our partners. It's really a plea for there to be attention paid to the context [in which we have sex] rather than the utterance of consent.

"So if you think you're lucky that he was nice to you during the encounter, and you never expected to have an orgasm or you never even really expected to have pleasure, then you're consenting to a really different act than someone else," she explained. But because we refuse to acknowledge the reality of bodily inequality, we rarely take this context into account.

What would looking at our sexual encounters with an eye for intimate justice—acknowledging bodily inequality—reveal? It might show that while men and women might be consenting to an equivalent number of sexual encounters, their average experience may differ widely due to their differing biology, which puts women more often in harm's way than it does men. And a better, more valid framework for understanding whether sex is ethical in these circumstances would need to take this fact into account.

Many of our conceptions of fairness assume the primacy of the will: "I want the world to be like this, and so it is." In some ways, so does our understanding of consent: "Men and women should be equivalent. We'll assume they are and treat them the same." But when it comes to the actual reality of sex, that understanding falls apart. And so does the legitimacy of consent as an adequate way to judge whether the sex we have is actually good.

. . .

No, ANATOMY ISN'T DESTINY, but it influences how we experience the world—and to some extent how we interact with it. Biological sex matters when we're talking about sex.

Gender matters too. Modern societies have started to challenge the meaning and importance of gender and gender roles;* after centuries of protest, even the staunchest traditionalists have begun to acknowledge that the ways in which gender has traditionally been understood tend to disadvantage women in particular and harm men in ways that are often overlooked. It's better to acknowledge, and celebrate, the range of human behavior: women don't always act one way, and men don't always act another.

But just because gender is socially conditioned and more flexible than we have acknowledged in the past does not mean that it no longer bears paying attention to—especially when we talk about sex.

In fact, it matters a lot, if for no other reason than that men and women still are socialized very differently and, as a result, bring those differences into their relationships, into how they experience them and what they expect from them.

In his book *The Utopia of Rules*, the late anthropologist David Graeber described how, in situations of structural inequality,

---

* "Sex" describes characteristics that are biologically defined, while "gender" refers to characteristics that are socially and culturally associated with biological sex.

the less powerful party works strenuously to figure out how the more powerful party might feel. The reverse is almost never true. Graeber gives the example of a popular creative writing exercise in which high school students are asked to describe a day from the perspective of the opposite sex. Girls write long and detailed essays that show they have already spent significant time thinking about the subject, while many boys simply refuse to write the essay at all.

Sex is still like that.

In our society, women are conditioned to take responsibility for the feelings of others, especially for men's. We teach women not to make a scene, not to be difficult, selfish, or rude, to modulate their behavior into what is socially acceptable. They're trained to get comfortable with their own discomfort. Despite various advancements, our actions are still shaped by centuries of embedded gender norms. And in some cases, even supposed solutions can be a double-edged sword. As contraception has become more mainstream and the risks of sex more diffuse, saying no can feel like less of an option for women: after all, what's your excuse? As employers dangle fertility assistance as a benefit and egg-freezing companies advertise their extended payment plans, it can become easy to forget that time is still passing, and allow ourselves to be strung along.

WOMEN HAVE MORE to lose from sex, and from a sexual culture gone wrong. Saying that this is the case should not be disempowering—it's simply the truth. Knowing the truth, rather than deceiving ourselves, gives us more power to make choices and decisions that really suit us. While we should be bold enough to reimagine the world as we like, we should also acknowledge the world that exists today.

All of this raises a question that has dogged feminists since the sexual revolution: Can women really consent to sex, under the coercive constraints of society and their own bodies? Categorically, yes. Women can and do consent to sex every day. Their choices are valid. Their partners are not necessarily taking advantage of them.

But what the complication of biology *does* suggest is that the ethic of consent—assuming as it does an equivalent freedom of choice between the two parties—is leaving some seriously unbalancing factors unaddressed. Thus consent, *just* consent, may not be enough to render sex ethical, or fair, or equally healthy for both participants.

And if we want a better sexual culture, that is what we should be striving for.

IN THE TWENTY-FIRST CENTURY, it often seems as though there's a binary choice: between regarding women as victims and regarding them as agents. Victimhood, of course, is bad. In that context, the question of whether to acknowledge the biological differences between men and women and what they mean for sex becomes a loaded one: Should we acknowledge female vulnerability and risk reinforcing women's subjugation, or should we pretend, optimistically, that all vulnerability has already been overcome?

Overcorrecting to avoid that victim status, some say that protecting women via law or norms (outside of basic consent) that take their vulnerabilities into account is patronizing. To do so presumes that women can't fight on their own, treats them like fragile creatures, and undermines their dignity. And drawing too much attention to the differences between the sexes, it is implied, would push women to see themselves as small, marginalized, and incapable. The immutability of biology already leaves women vulnerable, and men have forever lorded it over them. Why would we help it along?

Overcorrecting in another direction, the pro-agency approach agrees that we should not acknowledge these differences, and moreover should assume ourselves fully able to overcome them (with the help of the pill, ART, better childcare, etc.). With those at their disposal, women are able to take responsibility for whatever happens in their encounters and seek power regardless of any supposed inequality. This is true agency, and this will spring women from the victim trap.

But this victim/agent distinction is a bit suspect. It's selective and arbitrary. After all, we know that it would be nonsensical to say that treating people with equal respect for their dignity, despite their differences, reduces their agency. Laws and moral norms protect both men and women from theft, assault, and fraud, but it's rarely suggested that these laws turn men into victims. And if they did, would it be so bad?

Celebrated philosopher Martha Nussbaum writes: "Trauma and tragedy—the circumstances that create the basic framework of victimhood—force us to confront this dual nature of the human experience: we are at once agents of our own fate and vulnerable to the whims of a larger system over much of which we have no control."

She continues. "A *compassionate* society . . . is one that takes the full measure of the harms that can befall citizens beyond their own doing; compassion thus provides a motive to secure to all the basic support that will undergird and protect human dignity."

The binary choice between agency and victimhood is actually preventing us from establishing the foundation of basic human dignity that we need in order to build a society.

THE TRUTH THAT MEN AND WOMEN are different is frightening because of the worry that any difference discovered will be used as evidence of female inferiority. But things don't have to be this zero-sum. We can acknowledge inequalities and dedicate ourselves to treating each other well despite them. Women shouldn't have to surmount their biology as an obstacle in relationships, and what makes women women should not—logically or ethically— be seen as a liability. Different can just mean *different*, not worse. And difference can—and should—be respected. The dignity of women (and men) demands it.

Biological differences suggest that when sex is coercive, that coercion tends to runs in one direction: male to female. But norms and laws that respect vulnerability don't erode agency; rather, they create a framework within which women can develop and act as the fullest versions of themselves, with all of their realities taken into account. It's a better use of our energy to act on the basis of truth than to maintain that it doesn't or shouldn't exist.

Some truths about sex are quantifiable, like the easily observed biological differences between men and women. Others are less outwardly visible, but no less meaningful: truths about how much meaning we assign to the act regardless of intention, and how sexual encounters can affect us far more deeply than we might assume.

CHAPTER 5

Sex Is Spiritual

THE CLIENTELE IS ABOUT what you would expect for a mid-week nine a.m. at a downtown Le Pain Quotidien: loud talkers, mostly middle-aged men in suits and a few women in sensible sheath dresses, gesturing broadly over their lattes and blocking the aisles with their law firm–branded laptop bags.

It takes me a few seconds to locate Brooke in the back of the restaurant by the window, holding a latte of her own—bright yellow, turmeric.

"Sorry I'm late!" I huff—I had missed the bus in the rain and am fifteen minutes late for our interview.

"It's fine! My office is around the corner."

I first notice her stylish acrylic-framed eyeglasses, which

make my fogged-up tortoiseshells feel incredibly dated. They're a soft pink and a little cat-eyed, the perfect shape for her round, inviting face. Thirty years old, queer-identifying, she moved to DC from the West Coast and does advocacy work for a women's health organization. Brooke is a fast, organized talker—"I took some notes on the Metro to try to organize my answers"—but she still has a bit of SoCal vocal fry.

We're meeting to talk about her rape.

"I was raped in college," Brooke starts off confidently. "It was my sophomore year and it was someone that I was hooking up with. I had stated very clearly that I didn't want to have sex— we were both very drunk. I don't know, I guess I didn't want to have sex with someone until, you know, he was my boyfriend. But he was going down on me and then suddenly he was inside me."

Her voice is wobbling now.

"I remember thinking, 'Say out loud, "no," so at least you can tell people you said it.'"

We talk about the way her rape affected her. She's still working through it, which is part of the reason why she wanted to talk to me.

"Luckily, I didn't have that moment of 'This dirtied me or ruined me' in the way a lot of people who are religious do." She gives a suddenly brittle laugh.

"But there is still this sense that when someone is raped, that feels worse than if they're mugged. And I still stand by that. It's still a weapon of choice for men for that reason. Otherwise, they would just steal our new iPhone.

"Sometimes I try to grapple with the fact that the person who raped me didn't take anything from me. I was—I *am*—lucky that I didn't have an injury or pregnancy. . . . But I don't want to downplay or dismiss the real trauma behind it. I mean, it did cause PTSD that I still have to this day. And I had to have medication and therapy for so long."

Brooke pauses. Her voice is quieter now.

"Sex is just a very unique way we share our body with other people."

Sex Is Serious

We have tried to internalize the assumption that sex is an act just like any other, a pleasant bodily function with no intrinsic meaning or value. And yet we know that sexual assault is a crime *unlike* any other.

It's painful, but not difficult, to understand why. Rape is an intrusion onto—and into—the most private parts of our body. Sex comes close to who we are—we want to connect in the right way with people we care about; we don't want to be forced to connect with someone we do not choose. And because of lingering cultural connotations of defilement, that forced connection can feel particularly taboo.

Rape violates our bodily autonomy and compromises our self-sovereignty. It can alter our perception of ourselves, creating alienation where there once was none. For women, there is the fear of a forced or unwanted pregnancy. For both sexes, pain and diseases that could later prove deadly. After being sexually assaulted, both men and women often feel the need to reclaim themselves and their ability to have sex.

It's a common belief in religious traditions that our sexual encounters do in some way reach into the spirit. One Catholic priest suggested to a reporter at *The Atlantic* that as many as 80 percent of the people who came to him seeking exorcisms were sexual abuse survivors. In his theory, this particular kind of abuse can be so uniquely traumatic as to create the sort of "soul wound" that makes a person more susceptible to demonic possession.

And sexual assaults seem to outrage us more than most other crimes. Witness the Oregon father who in 2019 assaulted a university's Title IX official with a baseball bat—not for perpetrating a sexual assault but for mishandling his daughter's claim of one while at the official's school. The dad's attack was lawlessness—felony second-degree assault, in fact—to which the overwhelming public reaction was shrugged understanding, if not commiseration. "I mean . . . violence is not the answer, but I understand. I don't condone it, but I get it," read a typical comment on an online article discussing the case.

For whatever reason, it does seem that to be so intimately violated is understood as a distinctly terrible harm.

ON A PURELY RATIONAL BASIS, this feeling of seriousness makes perfect sense. Reproduction is a fundamental urge, one with the unique potential to create a new human life and one that—for women especially—creates extreme vulnerability. Any half-baked biologist who understands species propagation could explain why sex has an extreme payoff in terms of pleasure, and why in the heat of the moment we tend to be our most selfish and least self-reflective. The combination of great potential and chaotic desire creates a high-stakes situation every time, making sex something worth setting apart.

In the evangelical tradition in which I was raised, sexuality and desire were seen as holding an outsize power: a good marriage was basically essential for fulfillment and happiness, but sex was also something that could destroy you if done incorrectly, outside of marriage's sacred boundaries. According to the most vehement preachers, it was sinful, subject to a raft of prohibitions and hidden behind a veil of shame. (This is how many nonreligious people assume that Christians think about sex, and they're not always wrong.) While I escaped the worst of purity culture—the rings, the pledges, the stripping petals from a rose to symbolize the loss of value that comes from premarital sex—I was raised with the understanding that sex should be saved for marriage, on pain of . . . something.

Converting to Catholicism, I came to a more nuanced view. Sex *was* incredibly meaningful, but having it wasn't a sin. The capacity to both desire and experience pleasure was a human endowment; sexuality expressed our belonging to the embodied and biological world and was woven into our very fabric. According to the Catechism of the Catholic Church, sex is God given, carrying the power of love and (importantly) life. "It especially concerns affectivity . . . and in a more general way the aptitude for forming bonds of community with others." Our sexuality goes to the core of our person and is a fundamental part of our human existence. It allows us to form deep attachments to those with whom we share it and involves us in the joint creation of new life.

The Christian religion isn't the only one making these connections. Judaism does too. Sex is "an expression of the holiness of the created human body and human connection," according to Jewish studies professor and ethicist Rebecca Epstein-Levi, with a potential for both great risk and goodness. And this understanding of sex as a serious matter is not limited to just the Abrahamic or monotheistic traditions.

One of the Five Precepts, the moral underpinnings of Buddhism, is to refrain from sexual misconduct. Buddhist monks, like Catholic priests, are instructed to remain celibate, with the understanding that sex creates deep connections to the world and to other people. The Buddha tells one would-be monk, who has illicitly had sex with his own *wife*:

> Have I not taught the Dhamma in many ways for the sake
> of dispassion and not for passion; for unfettering and not
> for fettering; for letting go and not for clinging? Yet here,
> while I have taught the Dhamma for dispassion, you set
> your heart on passion; while I have taught the Dhamma
> for unfettering, you set your heart on being fettered; while
> I have taught the Dhamma for letting go, you set your
> heart on clinging.

In pagan religions, some traditions similarly hold sex to be a momentous act: a portrayal of the union of the highest deities. In traditional Wicca, sex is seen as a sacred joining, creating a strong spiritual bond. Even *Teen Vogue* has endorsed the power of "sex magic," advocating its use for manifesting the best possible reality in a way that nothing else can.

As my own understanding of sexuality evolved, I became more skeptical of the extremes. Yet there does seem to be something there: whether one is having sex or refraining from it, either way, sex is meaningful. It cannot be easily contained and should not be downplayed. We can't make it small.

In a sense, even the most restrictive Christian prohibitions on sex actually provide a positive vision of what sex can be—not just a mundane biological function conducted by fleshy bags of water and DNA, but something beautiful and profound that taps into our existence as human beings who are both "embodied spirits, inspirited bodies," as ethicist Margaret A. Farley puts it. Even if not every act of intercourse feels deeply meaningful, sex itself is a particular facet of our humanity connected to something deep within us and has the capacity to—literally—create the world anew.

All of this feels like a transgressive admission, because it puts the lie to our current social understanding that sex is just an activity like any other, one that can be managed casually, with our encounters having no intrinsic meaning or morality. But it is also true. Even with physical risks and potential for parenthood reduced, the gravity of sex somehow remains.

All or Nothing

Over the past several decades, our cultural narrative has gone a bit irrational on the question of sex, attempting to uphold two opposing opinions about what was once seen as obvious.

On the one hand, modern sexual liberals have mainstreamed the idea that sex means nothing, or at least not very much. Sexual desire is a physical, biological urge that is pleasant to fulfill—orgasms are nice!—and we don't need to read more into it than that.

You might think of it like skiing, or any other pleasurable but slightly risky physical pastime—extremely fun but generally devoid of external significance; a mostly individual pursuit that you can likely get better at with practice, one that can be done safely and without major consequences as long as you follow the rules: don't block the lifts, mind the slopes; get consent and use condoms.

On the other hand, our society has also come to the conclusion that sex means *everything*, or close to it. The sexual imperative is an overpowering force that should be liberated rather than constrained. Having an active sex life is a sign and symbol of health and—especially for women—a political statement signifying personal power and our liberation as a class, gender, or generation. Sex is key to the construction of our individual identities: we mull over our sexuality in public and in private, identifying ourselves by our orientations and affinities in the same way that we do by our race or nationality. Weighting it as such, we as a society construct increasingly elaborate sets of social and legal rules to make sure we're doing sex "right." Get consent, but make sure it's the right kind. Make sure the "yes" is affirmative, enthusiastic, provable in a court of law. And even though we have supposedly moved away from the older religious understandings of sex, our society still describes sexual assault as something that can destroy a man's or woman's world. Afterward, you exist as a "survivor" or—less optimistically—a victim.

It's difficult to see how all of these things can be true at the same time.

From Religion to Health

You might blame Freud for the confusion.

"In a normal vita sexualis no neurosis is possible," the Austrian psychoanalyst wrote in 1912. And even though many of his theories were later discredited to the point of comedy, his sexually preoccupied ethos has lived on to define what is normal and what is not. The prevailing takeaway from his work, which has since come to dominate American popular thinking, is that sexual repression causes a host of mental and emotional problems. So naturally, an active, liberated sex life is the necessary cure.

In the twentieth century, the power of religious institutions began to wane. New arbiters of morality emerged, ones that prided themselves on being scientific rather than superstitious. The fields of medicine and psychology became dominant, and the understanding of what was "good" moved from being shaped by morality to being shaped by science—to be "good" was now to be "healthy." And health, in turn, was shaped by what psychiatrists and physicians, society's new priests, considered normal or abnormal.

Freud, perhaps the most influential thinker of the twentieth century, believed that the human psyche was shaped by childhood sexuality. Healthy personality development depended on one's libido, or sexual energy, being channeled through various stages of psychosexual development properly and in the correct order. The id, ego, and superego revolved around obtaining pleasure (especially sexual pleasure) and mediating the desire for it. Sexual inhibition disordered one's psyche, and not having a robust, properly expressed sexuality led to problems of all kinds. As the sociologist Eva Illouz describes it, "Experts in the fields of psychology and psychoanalysis viewed the psychic history of the individual as being organized around sexuality, and in this respect, sexuality became an essential feature of what defined a person." The result? "Sexuality . . . became the sign and site of a 'healthy' self."

WHILE IT'S ALMOST *too* obvious to say that the way we think about sex is influenced by the culture and the time in which we live, understanding broader shifts does help explain how we got to where we are today. The relentless minimization of—and simultaneous obsession with—sex was the result of that shift from religion to health, combined with outsize social authority given to figures who were still figuring out their own work.

"Sex means nothing" was a negative response to the use of "traditional" sexual morality as a locus of control, one that prescribed life paths and defined behavior with coercive, puritanical force. The common narrative suggested that under the religiously informed, dangerously inhibited moral regime of the past, the act of sex itself was either a sin or close to it, procreation was its only purpose, and discussion of pleasure was taboo—the system itself was enforced by shame and stigma. Joyless prudery and inhibition ensued, along with female and LGBTQ oppression. Freedom became possible only with the introduction of a more scientific mindset, one that could discard the idea that sex had any inherent meaningfulness—science isn't concerned with morals, after all.

And its positive twin, the idea that "sex means everything," pushed back against the past from a different direction. It affirmed the twentieth century's revolutionary shift in view, one that equated morality with health, health with freedom from repression or inhibition, and full realization of one's self as the ultimate goal. If an active sex life was key to a healthy life, then sex was of huge importance. And luckily for us, we were now free to pursue it.

BUT AS BELIEFS to live by, both the "all" and the "nothing" understandings of sex veer wide of the mark.

For one thing, the idea of the past as an era of sexual repression and taboo is itself pretty recent and frequently misconstrued. The earliest Christians were radically gender egalitarian, even if later traditions took a more demonizing tone;* there were traditions of ecstasy in their religion, of desire as an inspiration. As for the now-commonplace assumption that our Victorian ancestors were repressed and socially silenced when it came to sex? They were *obsessed* with sex, even if they talked about it less in public.

The twentieth century's mania for demonizing inhibition had its own flaws, including what now seems to have been a wild underestimation of the necessity of some kinds of social and self-regulation. If the #MeToo moment showed us anything, it was that the sexual imperative can wreak havoc if left to run rampant. Sex has always been a socially constructed activity, with prescriptions and proscriptions around partners and timing. Cynically, one could say this was to better track lineages and paternities. More generously, one might admit that it was to keep our desires from spilling out of control and causing harm.

---

* At the end of the Roman Empire, the emergent sect of Christianity was distinguished in part by its unusual sexual mores, at least for the time period. In a society distinguished by a patriarchal hierarchy, a sharp distinction between the rights of citizens and noncitizens, and a large underclass of chattel slaves, expectations of female chastity—for respectable women, at least—were extremely high and inflexible. But for men of higher classes, there was an entirely different code: it was assumed that they could and should indulge their sexual desires as they pleased, with prostitutes (of which there were plenty), slaves of any kind, or anyone else who lacked the same social honor—nonpersons. Treating them as objects with which to satiate oneself was perfectly acceptable.

The apostle Paul, writing to fledgling communities of the Christian sect, wrote in opposition to porneia—prostitution and the buying and selling of people, male or female, as sexual objects. Contrary to the prevailing ethic of the times, this worldview suggested that all people, no matter which social class or sex, deserved to be treated with dignity rather than thought of as something to be consumed. "Neither slave, nor free, male, or female," Paul's description of humans in the view of the Christian God, was a subversive challenge to the entire Roman social order. Christianity became one of the great sources of the egalitarian tradition. Every person had a soul and thus had equal value.

It's possible, in fact, that the existence of centuries of tradition around sex—whether now perceived negatively or not—point to a truth: that sex is important, and uniquely so. Reducing the experience of sex to pure biology bypasses something that is also essential to it: meaning. Yes, sex and sexual desire are organic functions, but ones with enough resonance to be argued and debated, written and sung about, whispered over reverently and celebrated once community members come of age. Social norms often enforce the necessary limitations needed for communities to function. "Sex," as the philosopher Roger Scruton puts it, "is the bond of society and also the force that explodes it."

Sex Lingers

Given the profound nature of sex, it was clear why Brooke viewed her rape as a major instance of sexual violence, and why it had affected her for years afterward. There was something specific about the voiding of self-sovereignty around this particular act that seemed uniquely painful. But as the coffee shop emptied out and we continued to talk, it became clear that she, like many of us, had also had other unhappy sexual encounters. And though those encounters were consensual, the harms they caused weren't necessarily less significant.

"Not much was enjoyable for me in college," she said. "[Sex] was just what you did, because we all just wanted human contact and attention and to feel pretty. The men in these instances . . .

just making out wasn't enough. It was for me, but because they wanted more, I was like, 'Well, this is what adults do.'"

Even now, almost a decade later, she pointed out that she and many of her friends still often ended up doing the same thing. "I don't want to have sex with you, but I'm doing it because, like, I have to be"—she laughs dryly—"polite."

Brooke talked about how she had recently become more comfortable with hooking up with men she met on apps. She saw it as a necessary reclaiming of her own agency and sexuality after disappointing past experiences. But upon reflection, she was less sure that it was addressing what really hurt. The sex, she acknowledged, wasn't even pleasurable. She wondered whether supposedly "casual" sex was actually playing a mixed role for the other women she knew, most of whom had also had similar experiences—not rape, probably, but sex that they didn't necessarily want to have. Were they seeking out sexual encounters because they wanted them, or because they were avoiding something—their thoughts, their histories, their bodies, their insecurities; loneliness, limitations, or even just quiet?

"Really," Brooke mused, "we're all depressed and we need therapy . . . but instead we're overcompensating."

Consent Doesn't Compensate

Even consensual encounters can fail to respect the profundity that we sense sex holds. Blogger Ella Dawson defines "bad sex" as "the sex we have that we don't want to have but consent to anyway." She writes:

> Bad sex can leave you feeling violated, sick, confused. There isn't anyone to blame: no one forced anyone to participate. You could have said no and you didn't. You didn't have the words or you didn't have the courage to say them. . . . It doesn't necessarily traumatize you, but it can stick with you, a moment of embarrassment or regret. You try not to think about it, do your best to brush it off, maybe even joke about it with your friends the next day at brunch.
>
> Too much of the time, bad sex is the norm for young women, not the exception.

Brooke made it clear that she had had good sexual encounters too, and that she didn't consider either her rape or her less pleasant instances of consensual sex to be insurmountable harms. But what she said about needing to cope, finding ways to compensate for the depressing-ness of those encounters, tracked with the conversations I had with other women and men, and the ones that had been highlighted by the #MeToo movement at large. There was rape, a distinct thing, but there was also something else—agreed-to encounters that were still negative. The harms of those experiences might be less severe than those from an outright rape, but they seemed similarly immiserating, because sex tends to retain that same significance in almost every situation—that long-understood, traditionally revered connection with our emotions, our values, our sense of self and understanding of the world around us.

Consent is meant to separate criminal sex from noncriminal sex and sexual assault from everything else. But consent doesn't address the gravity of what sex is or how it affects us. Consent only asks if we have said yes or not; if yes, it assumes that the sex we then start having is good. But it's often not, and it can damage us to the precise depths that sex reaches within us.

The "bad sex" that is put up with because it's not rape, the casual encounters that we dismiss as "just sex," can be emotionally and psychologically alienating. Even agreed-to sex can separate us from our own deepest desires and pleasures, and from the sense of identity that comes from acting in the world in accordance with our own wants, rather than someone else's.

Georgetown law professor Robin West coined the term *hedonic dysphoria* to categorize the harms that she believes are caused by unwanted sex, specifically by unwanted sex in a culture where consent is the ruling arbiter of good.

We know, West says, that sex is supposed to be intimate and good, that it has a certain meaningfulness to it, and that when our experiences frequently fail to match up with what we know to be true, we can feel it. It matters. But we also assume, based on the prevailing ethic of consent, that consensual transactions are good, pleasurable, and valuable because of their consensual nature. We should feel happier and more fulfilled and less violated, because we *did* agree to them.

So what about the many instances of sex we have experienced where these beliefs don't line up? The results are a close match to the painful confusion that Dawson describes and the deep discomfort that Brooke intuits in herself and her peers. It creates a jarring disconnect between what we believe about how we should be experiencing the world and the way in which we actually are.

Sex like this reinforces the notion that our bodies aren't our own, that they exist to serve someone else's desires rather than ours. We trivialize ourselves and our importance in the world, accepting as truth the feeling that our own desires, pleasures, or pains should not and will not determine our choices and our outcomes. We objectify ourselves, often in the ugliest way. Those invalidations don't cease to exist just because we said yes—some of them may even be amplified.

"[A] woman or man who experiences [consensual sex as bad]," West writes, "faces the possibility not just of 'regret,' but of a lack of alignment between the experiences of their physical selves, and the societal expectation of the nature of that experience."

"The distrust is of not just "experience,'" she continues, "but the experiences of one's own physical body, and more specifically, of one's own hedonic self. The result is a psychic and a physical gaslighting."

You might then be brave enough to question society. Or, you just ignore the truth your body and soul are telling you— distancing from yourself, accepting what shouldn't be accepted. And how many of us do that?

Advocating against rape is necessary and crucial. But in our eagerness to communicate that sexual violence is unacceptable, we can overlook the less obvious, but just as meaningful, ways in which even consensual sex can cause harm. Yet the significance of both kinds of harm—from rape or from "bad" consensual sex—is evidence that sex comes close to who we are, and to how we connect. Sexuality is uniquely meaningful to human beings, as a millennium's worth of tradition and our own intuitions show.

Sex is big. It's creative. It allows for the pleasures (or pains) of intimacy that we often desperately seek. At times, it is an opening into our souls, one that has the potential to touch and change who we are. We shouldn't forget that sex is serious. But too often, we do.

As OUR CONVERSATION wound down, Brooke seemed to anticipate the most common pushback to her and other women's complaints about the felt harms of consensual sex. Sex may be profound *for you*, but not for me. Consent may not be perfect, but the responsibility is on *you* to speak up if you feel uncomfortable. And yet she suggested that that couldn't be the end of it.

"I still feel like all of this is still about how women can be better about expressing their own boundaries and also removing themselves when a boundary is crossed. But I would love to just have fewer instances where I have to do that. I'm getting better about doing it, but if I'm removing myself from ten instances, those are still ten instances where someone else is crossing important boundaries. And maybe ten years ago I wouldn't have removed myself or it would have been worse."

Personal growth is an improvement but—as Brooke implies—not one that scales. How do we do better as a society, not just as individuals?

CHAPTER 6

Our Sex Lives Aren't Private

TINDER LAUNCHED ITS FIRST major branding campaign in 2018. I remember seeing the red flame logo and the offensively cheery photo sets all around Washington, DC, plastered on bus shelters and bike docks and lining the walls of the Metro. Conspicuously attractive models grinned down at me as I juggled coffees and dodged traffic while walking to my downtown office. Trendy Zennials eating cake (always cake! why so much cake?!) winked at me as I tripped over the rental scooters that were always, somehow, in the middle of the sidewalk.

Called "Single, Not Sorry," the campaign featured— according to Tinder's marketing kit—"hero women dating the way they want to." There were hypercolored photos of cool girls in a retro roller rink, disco-skating under neon lights. Couples (or, I suppose, not-couples) climbed chain-link fences in the dawn light in romantic defiance of NO TRESPASSING signs. Sexy swipers laughed with friends at greasy-but-chic late-night diners, surrounded by a bevy of potential partners.

With taglines like "Single does what single wants" and "Single never has to go home early," the swipe-dating pioneer was building on what has always been held out as the promise of dating apps: no rules, no critics, and lots of options. After all, how we have sex is an expression of our individuality. And how we choose to fulfill our desires is no one's business but our own.

FROM ANCIENT HISTORY until approximately 2009, most couples met in the same way—they relied on their families and local social circle to find mates for the purpose of family formation and long-term partnership. But in the first decade of the twenty-first century, everything changed. Computer algorithms—the OkCupid quiz, the eharmony survey, whatever evil demon lives inside the Hinge app—replaced human matchmakers. Rather than having our friends and relatives involved in choosing our partners, we turned it into a private job.

At peak churn, Kate—a strategy consultant in her midthirties—was on three different apps and averaged four to five dates a week. "I had a little bit of a private-equity metaphor," she revealed to me. "My pipeline, my due diligence, my holding period for the investment, and then how quickly I exit the investment—you know, how much time am I going to invest in them, and am I chatting with someone who's just going to disappear? And when are you exiting because you've gotten everything you're going to get out of it? I think my most common holding period was one date—very few people move to a second."

Kate kept a spreadsheet of her dates' various characteristics—age, location, education, looks—and other useful information. "It all sounds very extractive but . . . I felt like time was ticking away and maybe the right person was out there but was going to be scooped up by someone else, and apps were where all the people were. And on there it felt like the only way to go was a high-volume strategy. It was fairly exhausting and I don't think it made me happy, but I also felt like I didn't really have a choice."

Stanford University sociologist Michael Rosenfeld, who has been compiling data on how couples meet for the past decade, estimates that 2013 was the year in which online dating overtook meeting through friends as the most common way for heterosexual couples to get together, with swipeable dating apps specifically on the bleeding edge of that shift. More recently, this growth was turbocharged by the COVID-19 pandemic, when lockdowns combined a realization of one's own isolation with a literal inability to get out and meet other people. Almost all of the major dating apps saw double-digit user growth in 2020.

IF WE NOW see sex as personal and private—something that is and should be shaped solely by our own desires—dating apps in particular are sold as the apotheosis of our current sexual ideal. Two people—that is, two individual sets of preferences—seek each other out, satisfy their appetites, and go their own ways (or maybe even stay together), unburdened and free from the prying gazes of parents, teachers, church leaders, or an overly curious government. Apps like Tinder seemingly make it possible for two consenting adults to get together, get what they want, and go, while their activities remain completely self-contained.

The apps (and their regular-old-website predecessors) do deliver on at least some of that promise. They *are* private, or at least much more private than asking your mom, church, or coworkers to set you up with a date. You have wide latitude to look for exactly what you want without being judged for it. And now that you're swiping through a pool of millions instead of your own limited list of contacts, it's possible to imagine you might actually be able to find it.

The level of privacy that online dating offers has meaningful upsides: sexual minorities can pursue who they like with a lesser sense of fear or shame; apps and sites are more likely to connect couples with different racial, educational, or geographic backgrounds. But at the same time, privacy also means that no one is holding you to account, for better or for worse. On the internet, as the saying goes, no one knows that you're a dog . . . or that you're not a natural blond, or that you didn't actually go to Yale, or that you're only six-foot-three when you're standing in front of a trick mirror at a state fair. You're also at liberty to choose and act as you see fit: you can find someone who likes the same sex acts that you do, someone who follows the same obscure bands, someone who is also searching for the best taco in the city (that's everyone, apparently), or none of the above. You can be rude, you can be crude, you can ghost, and no one in your circle of *actual* acquaintances will ever know unless you choose to tell them. No one can see your messages or your dick pics. No one will know what you get up to when (or if) you do meet up.

The promise of today's dating world is confidentiality and nonjudgment. Being the only counsel for our affairs allows us to optimize for our own private preferences without interference. Our sex and dating lives can exist in a vacuum, free from the limitations of others' expectations. But the reality—of both our desires and what dating by these means can deliver—is more complicated.

Inventing Privacy

"Privacy" is a modern invention. For most of human history, people lived together in small, intensely interdependent communities. Everyone but the extremely wealthy—or the monastic religious—shared close quarters. Radical independence was difficult, if not impossible, and there was no expectation that any part of one's life could or should be off limits to other people. That included sex.

Because, both practically and philosophically, why would it be? Sex was fundamental to communities—it was how they were formed, how they expanded, and how they reproduced themselves over time. Sex between a man and woman could unite warring clans. The Trojan War was fought over a missing wife.

In the Middle Ages, public "bedding" rituals for newlyweds

were not uncommon, drawing friends, family, and the public at large into a married couple's sexual relationship. Nosy neighbors monitored sexual unions and could report bad behavior to churches and courts. Rather than surveillance being seen as an invasion, the presence of others was simply accepted as a dimension of sexual intimacy. Relational upset could have far-reaching outcomes, after all. And even attempted "private" behavior often led to public outcomes that were difficult to avoid. Sex tended to lead to pregnancy, and it's hard to hide a baby, especially if— as most people did until after the Industrial Revolution—you lived in a small community and depended on your membership within it to get by. Your business was everyone else's, and thus everyone else had a say—or at least could keep track of what was going on. The decision to sleep with someone else could rarely be confined to just the two individuals involved.

Until, that is, the twentieth century.

In 1890, American lawyers Samuel D. Warren and (future Supreme Court justice) Louis D. Brandeis published an article entitled "The Right to Privacy" in the *Harvard Law Review*, in which they argued for "the right to be let alone":

> Of the desirability—indeed of the necessity—of some
> such protection, there can, it is believed, be no doubt. . . .
> The intensity and complexity of life, attendant upon
> advancing civilization, have rendered necessary some
> retreat from the world, and man, under the refining
> influence of culture, has become more sensitive to
> publicity, so that solitude and privacy have become

more essential to the individual; but modern enterprise and invention have, through invasions upon his privacy, subjected him to mental pain and distress, far greater than could be inflicted by mere bodily injury.

They weren't writing about sexual privacy in particular. (Although, interestingly, the idea for the article came about after newspapers and photographers had had a bit too much fun documenting the wedding of Warren's daughter.) But their paper caused a fundamental shift in legal theory, and in our understanding of what a normal and preferred level of seclusion should look like in modern life.

Brandeis had died by 1965, but the U.S. Supreme Court maintained an interest in protecting privacy in the midst of the sexual revolution. Ruling in the case of *Griswold v. Connecticut*, the court established a right to "marital privacy" while overturning the state of Connecticut's ban on the use of contraceptives. The idea of sex as a fundamentally private act between two married parties—not one that should be subject to public or communal judgment or restrictions—would soon be expanded to include the unmarried, too. And the shift from public to private, in sex *and* social expectations, has only gained steam since.

Today, privacy is seen as necessary for developing personhood and autonomy; even as a precondition for forming one's identity. And we think of sex as a particularly personal, private activity, focused on our individual bodies, preferences, and modes of pursuing pleasure. Thanks to the pill and its contraceptive descendants, we can generally avoid any too-public mistakes or consequences, and what we do doesn't have to have any effect on anyone else. Unlike the rest of our lives, sex can exist in a vacuum.

Except, of course, that that isn't quite true.

We may think that our actions are self-contained, independent, and a function only of our personal desires. But no one speaks a private language, not even in our private interactions. Our sex lives are still socially constructed: how we talk about sex, what we expect from our interactions with each other, and how we behave. Far from being in a self-contained bubble, we are enacting communal dynamics and relationships when we have sex; our individual desires are often channeled through and into an existing set of cultural molds. And though we would like to think that our individual actions affect only us, we are in fact building and reinforcing narratives that we go on to spread. We define what sex means for those around us, too.

Privatizing Sex

AT THE TIME that the "Single, Not Sorry" ad campaign was being rolled out, I was single and feeling more than a little sorry for myself. I was on the apps, of course, but begrudgingly. I had never quite achieved the blissful level of cake-eating autonomy that they seemed to encourage, and coming off a long-term relationship and staring down my thirties, I wasn't really looking for the fly-by-night hookup experience that many of them held up as the ideal. While the apps were ostensibly "dating" apps, they weren't necessarily geared toward finding a relationship as such. After all, they made money when people stayed swiping.

Tinder and its siblings did allow me to test the waters as I fumbled my way back into singledom. It was comforting, in a way, to know that news of my awkward first dates wouldn't make it back to my ex or his friends, or that if I wanted to, I could hook up with a random stranger and make it as though it had never happened. I could go on dates with whatever kind of person I wanted to (at least, if they matched with me) and not have to defend their weird traits—or worse, my confused attraction to said weird traits—to anyone. Still, I came to crave a little mediation; there was something about the experience that toggled between too many options and too little control. Meeting someone through friends—or even at work, in my neighborhood, somewhere where it didn't quite seem like me versus a million randoms with no real reason to care—began to look better and better.

My ambivalence wasn't uncommon, I found out.

"One night I kind of just wanted to hook up," said Madeline, a young woman I spoke with in DC. "I was texting a guy on Tinder and then I was just like, 'Do you want to come over?' I remember texting my friends and saying I ordered a man on Tinder for delivery!" Madeline had grown up in California but went to college in the South. Most of the friends she had gone to school with had married in their early twenties, but she, at twenty-nine, was in no hurry to settle down. In fact, she reveled in the fact that she had slipped the leash of expectations and had moved to Los Angeles.

"It felt like I was making the hookup about what I wanted, trying to own that I'm also capable of wanting no-strings-attached sex. And that felt powerful. He drove from Silver Lake to Santa Monica, which is pretty far away." She paused, considering what she had just said. "Obviously I was joking about the delivery thing. Obviously! And he ended up being a friend with benefits for a while. But I wonder if when there's so many people in front of you—a profile is, like, a picture and three words—it's making us dehumanize each other. Like, you feel you don't have to care about the person, right? Because, you know, they're one of a million. They're physically and literally on your phone one of a million."

Madeline's comment—unusual in its frankness but not in the feelings it conveyed—summed up some of the contradictions presented by the independent, privatized sort of relationships that apps had made the norm. The choice to have sex, how, and with whom, was all hers. Unlike the closely watched friends she grew up with, her relationships, sex life, and marriage (or lack thereof), were all hers, springing from her personal desire and not subject to anyone else's approval. And the sex itself was pretty well contained. Her Tinder delivery, whom she saw a few times and then dispatched, didn't seem to have a meaningful effect on the rest of her life. He was into it, she was into it, then they stopped, and presumably they caused no harm.

At the same time, why was "no-strings-attached sex" the kind of sex she wanted? And was it, even? Why did she describe it the way that she did, with a flippancy that gave even her pause when she repeated it aloud? Despite the seemingly self-contained nature of her dating life, she wondered, justifiably, about how it bled into other parts of life. How did having sex in that way change her mindset? What about everyone else's? In the moment, her hookup felt like it had taken place in a sort of bubble—a private space of desire fulfilled. But had it?

Plus, there were ways in which existing in that bubble might be slightly less delightful than she had assumed. "He also could have murdered me, I guess," she mused at one point, correctly noting that these self-contained encounters left little space for accountability.

For Madeline, privacy was valuable as a space for self-discovery. And yet she had also identified some of its distinctive dangers. The most obvious, of course, being that having no one know anything about your life—where you go, whom you're with, what kind of person they are—is often nonideal. It's a trade-off that in modern life can be somewhat mitigated—just call an Uber if things get weird!—but still opens the door to an adverse outcome, be it an uncomfortable few hours or an actual assault.

According to Rosenfeld's study, 90 percent of couples who started their relationships online had no other connections to each other—when the research was published, the title of the study was "Disintermediating Your Friends" But this privatization of sex can introduce challenges. As Lori Gottlieb told me, "With people who are friends before—those relationships tend to have more longevity. But even if they don't work out, it tends to end better for both people. Because there's still that glue of 'I see you as a person. I know you as a person. And I want to be really careful with you.'"

But with dating on the apps, she said, their worlds don't collide. "The community used to be the Greek chorus. 'You don't do this. This is what we do. These are our ethical rules.' If you have a bunch of mutual friends, you know you're going to be really careful about how you act because there are certain standards in the community around us. But usually when people meet on apps, they don't overlap. The people are total strangers to each other. You can do whatever you want to do. And no one can call you on it because you don't have any mutual friends."

In the past, meeting someone through friends and community gave something of an incentive for good, or at least socially acceptable, behavior. The relative lack of privacy that used to come with dating on, say, a college campus provided at least a level of minor regulation—sometimes grating but often welcome. Texting to set up a date with a friend of a friend, one could be fairly assured that one wouldn't be sent an unsolicited picture of his penis, because that sort of gross behavior would get around. Whisper networks meant that people would hear about it and the offender would likely face some sort of stigma, or at least other women might know to be more cautious. An untoward or dangerous sexual preference might be held in check, simply through the knowledge that judgment from others might someday arrive. But in a world of thinned-out connection, to whom can one turn when things go wrong?

"Seeking to 'free' sexual love from its old communal restraints," writes philosopher and poet Wendell Berry, "we have 'freed' it also from its meaning, its responsibility, and its exaltation. And we have made it more dangerous."

Whose Idea?

When it comes to the sort of independence that the apps advertise (and that the modern world fetishizes), we have actually bought into an illusion: that the choices we're making—in favor of autonomy, privacy, and extreme flexibility—are themselves independently arrived at, that this particular preference has emerged fully out of the vacuum of our own personality. Yet (and sorry in advance for getting meta) even our own vision of the level of privacy we desire is itself not independently constructed. It's still shaped by a larger, communal norm that we didn't necessarily choose for ourselves.

CAPITALISM FRAMES OUR modern lives so completely that we're liable to forget that it's even there. We're trained to think that everything can be traded and logically should be: time, desire, ideas, and even selves are viewed through the lens of transaction. The ultimate goal is to maximize your personal achievement and private gain; anything that blocks the path to increased consumption is a waste of time, or at least a questionable use of your resources.

The logic of the market has become a totalizing force, and everything—including our supposedly private experience of sex—is shaped by it. (What else is "ordering a guy on Tinder" except a person and experience repackaged as a commodity for consumption on demand?)

Our wholesale adoption of Tinder and its fellow apps are the culmination of this mindset, the prime example of capitalism invading our theoretically privately chosen practices of sex and dating. Madeline's description of her hookup as a "delivery" wasn't an entirely personal choice; the app explicitly portrayed him as one product among many to choose from, and the advertised choice to swipe right on him as an expression of sex-positivity and personal empowerment. It shaped her language and mindset. Just because we manage to keep our individual actions to ourselves (relatively; let's not get into how much information we give out by dating online: everything from our pre-date Googles to the destinations of our three a.m. Lyfts) doesn't mean that we have arrived at our mindsets by ourselves. Whether it's *Buzz-Feed* editors trying to get clicks by writing listicles about the best dating stories or Tinder engineers in Silicon Valley encouraging users to stay on the app just a little longer, there is incentive for people without our best interests at heart to both instill and encourage certain ways of being, and to exploit vulnerabilities we already have.

Still, one of the defining features of capitalism is its focus on the untethered individual. "The one central and indispensable axiom of metaphysical capitalism is 'I am my own,'" writes Alan

Jacobs, distinguished professor of the humanities at Baylor University. "I am a commodity wholly owned and operated by myself in service to my own interest, as defined by me. I am my own store of capital." But even the preference for complete independence is not necessarily one we've arrived at on our own. This vision of the human person makes possible a perfectly flexible, endlessly interchangeable set of workers and consumers. But this vision of the human person is a windfall to the economy and the companies that make it up, which can count on us to buy their products and commit our lives to the work of making and selling them. The ideal of the hypermobile, hyperliquid existence is not necessarily one today's young adults have arrived at on our own.

And despite our pretensions to privacy and independence, this externally imposed shaping happens on multiple levels. Dating apps position themselves as fun tools, freeing us up to meet new people and explore preferences we might never have known we had. Potential dates are cards in a deck; connecting with others is reduced to a game.

But at the same time as app users are invited to commoditize others, we're urged to do the same to ourselves: curating, packaging, and assessing our own worth according to the digital marketplace and alienating ourselves in the process. Even as we pick through other people, we are wondering how to best sell ourselves to strangers according to the rules of supply and demand. Transactionalism breeds transactionalism, rather than the kind of connection that the majority of people using apps to find a partner actually seek.

. . .

A CERTAIN LEVEL of transactionalism has always been present in our common understanding of sex. Women (and men)
were given in marriage to cement family and tribal bonds; marriage itself was a way to exchange property and ensure its orderly
transmission across generations through the creation of legiti-
mate heirs. Those medieval bedding ceremonies were publicly
observed so that the economic or social benefits of a marital
union could be guaranteed for the families who brokered it.

But in the modern era, the economic view has been fully privatized, despite the fact that we still view this past vision of marriage as constraining and unromantic. And it's almost purely in
the service of capital; it's no longer even justified by the idea of
helping our families or communities thrive.

The early 2000s saw the public acceptance of the "sexual
economics" theory of psychology, which posited that men's and
women's sexual behavior followed the principles of economic exchange, with sex as a resource women had for sale. Pickup-artist
culture helped to popularize the extreme marketization of sex,
teaching men formulas for how to quantify and rank women by
their "sexual market value." In the process, of course, they dehu-
manized both the women to whom the 1–10 scale applied and
the men who used it to distance themselves from feeling. The
economics-text dating guides that began to flood bookstores in
the 2010s—*Date-onomics; Data, a Love Story; Find a Husband
After 35 Using What I Learned at Harvard Business School* (a
real title)—were perhaps less nefarious in motive, but they also

didn't help. Today, dating can seem more like a competition than an attempt to build a relationship or form a connection.

Which makes sense. The capitalist ideal that has formed our understanding of "independence" tends to preclude connection and solidarity in favor of the possibility of private gain. The fierce privacy and optionality that we idolize can tend toward dehumanization and alienation, and there is no outside mediator to appeal to when things don't seem quite right.

IF MADELINE'S ABILITY to order a private "delivery" and laugh about it with her friends helped her view Tinder in a positive light—even with some misgivings—Sam's experience was its flip side. "I go on the apps," he said, "but every time I go on them, I feel this sense of loneliness and emptiness descend upon me. It's terrible. It's gotten worse over the years." The odd thing about Sam was that he wasn't hurting for sex. In fact, he was one of the more successful app users I had met. And yet even his own experience of optionality and independence was delivering diminishing returns.

"I see all these people who I would love to meet," he said. "But chances are, you're not going to match with most of the people you swipe right on.

"Sometimes there's people who really stand out, you look at their bio, and you're like, 'This person has everything that I'm looking for.' But that also feels terrible. Because again you're like, 'Chances are, I'm never gonna meet this person. And I'm also competing with three hundred other guys who also think the same thing about her.' And I find that completely soul crushing and actually kind of depressing."

If we are fully independent, we have to assume that no one else is looking out for us; they're looking out for themselves instead. Individualism allows the chance to make of yourself what you will—there is no one you should feel indebted to and no one holding you back—but also puts the burden for success on you alone. And there is something about one's individual worth being up for judgment by a crowd of strangers, decontextualized and torn from meaningful context, that feels more painful than flush with possibility. The feeling of being one faceless, frequently rejected contender among many now occurs on an unprecedented scale.

THE MODERN ERA'S emphasis on individualism has given us the freedom to try new things, to escape unwanted surveillance. But it can also open us up to degradation and to the further entrenchment of past harm. Abuse can be hidden or left uninterrogated as someone's private "kink." Racism, not naturally occurring but entrenched through centuries of practice, is internalized as simply personal preference. If everything is an individual's private choice, there remains little opportunity to teach, to positively shape, or even simply to question preferences that do, in fact, deserve scrutiny. By pretending there is no system connecting us, we give up the opportunity to correct it.

Capitalism itself is a largely amoral system. And it's an odd lens through which to view our social—let alone most intimate—relationships. Most of us hope that sex will be more than a bloodless exchange of property. Relationships aren't simply an exchange of goods and services. But when we view sex in isolation, as a private activity engaged in to satisfy our own desires, it becomes easier to forget that those outside of us—*our partners*—are human, too.

Independence can go from freeing to alienating with unexpected speed. And that atomization can hurt. Our dating practices may have overcorrected in the direction of privacy; what we need now is a realization that a positive sexual culture involves more than just the two most immediate actors. Including others in our relationships may improve them.

The question, then, is whom to include. Our desires, our practices, even our values are more susceptible to outside influence than we thought. We should wonder who's doing the influencing, and why—and what exactly it's doing to us. Just because a particular sex act, or even lifestyle, was chosen doesn't mean that it was come by independently. It also doesn't mean that it won't ripple outward, which suggests that our friends, families, and broader communities maybe *do* have a real stake in our sex lives. Sex is less private than we think it is—a good reason to think more clearly about the norms we are wittingly or unwittingly putting into place.

Sure, "Single does what single wants." But what if "what single wants" is wrong?

CHAPTER 7

Some Desires Are Worse Than Others

I WAS AT a mid-December holiday party in DC, crushed up in the dimly lit kitchen of a rented group row house. The room managed to be simultaneously sweaty hot and icy cold; it depended on whether you were standing near the stove, where the dregs of a pot of "mulled wine" continued to stew on a gas burner that seemed destined to set someone's hair on fire, or by the back door, where a cluster of stylish foreign correspondents (one of the last groups for whom smoking still seems to signify cool) were rotating in and out to huddle over cigarettes.

The host had run out of brandy for the wine early in the night, and, we later found out, had been dosing the mixture with straight vodka since ten p.m.—meaning that by around midnight, with beer running low and concentrated wine substance ιne main beverage on hand, things had taken a turn for the sloppy and confessional.

"So here's a thing," said Kirsten, a videographer I'd never met before, over the drunken din. She had chestnut hair, a rare set of extremely successful bangs, and an open, cheerful midwestern face. "I've been going on dates with this guy who I really like."

She went on to describe him as she pulled me into a nook just off the kitchen, slightly away from the crowd. The guy was funny, handsome, and smart, with an impressive job, all the sorts of things you'd want to hear a new friend tell you about her latest romantic prospect.

"But he chokes me during sex?"

She didn't really like the choking, Kirsten explained, but she really liked *him*. She wasn't sure whether to say anything, or even if it could actually be considered a valid problem. After all, sex like this was something that she'd said yes to; and she had definitely said yes to him—it was the bargain one made in order to leap off the dating app carousel into the arms of an otherwise great guy. And anyway, this kind of thing had happened to her friends too—the norm for heterosexual hookups seemed to have changed. Vanilla was out, extremes were to be expected.

"I mean, what do you think? Is that okay?"

No Judgment

Kirsten was asking me, a perfect stranger, for permission to complain about being surprise-choked by a sexual partner because she wasn't sure that she was allowed to otherwise. The taboo on questioning someone else's sexual preference was that strong. And yet it was also clear that this particular desire (and the casual assumption that it would be accepted with delight) disturbed her—and frankly, it disturbed me, too.

In the contemporary era, we blithely list off our sexual preferences like items on a menu, staunchly refusing to believe that they might reflect on our personal psychology or be shaped by the culture around us. Desire is desire—immutable and unimpeachable. "You do you" is a truism. We are loath to criticize any sexual choice, as long as all parties have agreed to take part.

"Between two consenting adults" has become a stock phrase, a conversational YIELD sign indicating that whatever is detailed next might raise eyebrows but must remain beyond critique. It's a matter of respect and a sign of enlightenment to accept the sexual proclivities of others, no matter how bizarre. For those hoping to gain a partner, it might even be a matter of prudence (given the options, you take what you can get). But it isn't clear that the growth of uncritical sex positivity is as *positive* a development as it has been made out to be. Sex is not amoral. Some desires are worse than others. Yet the bias toward unquestioning acceptance makes it difficult to say so, even when something feels obviously wrong. Because apart from nonconsent, is it possible for anything to *be* wrong?

The critic Michael Sacasas has written about how modern Western societies have come to think about desire, compared with other cultures and traditions. Generally speaking, he thinks, "we're less likely to judge our desires negatively or conclude that

..ney ought to be deferred, circumscribed, or even possibly denied." It's not a particularly attractive stance, when stated baldly—in fact it reeks of self-centeredness. But we have built a web of justifications for it, ones that we are willing to state aloud and ones that we tend not to want to acknowledge, even to ourselves.

Some of these justifications are admirably openhearted. An increased appreciation of intersectionality has led to the understanding that lived experience is shaped in different ways by race, gender, and class, making people who are committed to equal rights justifiably wary of endorsing universal prescriptions. Having adopted the "born this way" ethos to support LGBTQ rights in particular, many of us are loath to pull back and suggest that desire is mutable. We don't want to suggest that some orientations might be a choice, and risk those groups' marginalization. We are uncomfortable imposing our personal views on others; in a free society, morality is seen as a private affair.

Other justifications are a predictable result of an increasingly capitalist, market-logic culture—"the very principle of which is that what we want, we should have," in Sacasas's words. We're urged to fully explore our inclinations and multiply our paths to personal fulfillment. But to question the primacy of desire would eventually mean suggesting that some forms of sexual expression are better or worse than others, or harmful even if they're consented to. It feels like a slippery slope. We don't want to judge other people's desires for fear of being judged ourselves. Who will get to decide what's allowed and what's not? Whose desires will be disapproved? Will they be ours? These are not easy questions to answer, and a consumerist culture has trained us to jealously guard access to all of our options. Any boundary is seen as a threat.

But at the heart of many justifications is an unwillingness to be inconvenienced in any real way. We fear being asked to look too closely at our own desires. We are wary of being pressed to acknowledge what they say about us or what impact they might have on others. Because if we agree that some things are normatively good or bad, that some acts are morally acceptable and others are always wrong, or that some preferences and appetites might be unhealthy, that would mean that we might have to do "good" things that we don't want to do, or might no longer be able to do the "bad" things we enjoy. We might have to acknowledge that we could be better than we are. We might have to change.

THE CONSENT PARADIGM gives us a way out of this discomfort, or at least makes it easier for us to stick to a position of moral neutrality. In the contemporary era we have settled upon consent as a lowest common denominator that we can all agree on. Once we see that it is established, consent functions as an iron curtain, a social and political divider that cuts our experiences in half.

We use it to separate our intimate lives into those parts that are up for discussion and those that are seen as exempt from critique. But in allowing consent to be that divider, we have arbitrarily—and incorrectly—set many of our deepest tensions and disagreements behind a veil.

Consent has helpfully given us a way of dodging difficult

\...estions about morality and autonomy, but they are unhealthy ones to dodge. Because some things *are* worse than others, or at least should not be mainstreamed, and we should be able to say so. It should not be so hard to express our own discomfort and discuss the broader implications of various preferences and practices, whether it's the long-term impacts of sex work, the psychological underpinnings of BDSM, or the downsides of casual sex. But in a world of uncritical sex positivity, our ability to critique is limited.

When we *do* want to object to a particular act or practice, often the best we can do is frame it as not a moral failing but a failure of consent. And we try, within our constraints, to make space for these complaints by saying that the consent given wasn't real: not *really* affirmative or not enthusiastic, even if enthusiasm was performed. In our limited language for critique, the only bad things are those that weren't consented to, which can maybe include things that were consented to but in truth were unwanted: sexual acts agreed to in order to "hold up one's end of the bargain," to please a pushy partner, or to avoid something worse.

But this is the problem with consent: it leaves so much out. Practices that are consensual can still be damaging; the absence of consent is not the only indicator of problematic sex. Consent alone ignores that we can say yes to something that is harmful to us or others. These situations are often consented to by any average person's understanding of the word; what would be better would be to understand them as being consented to, perhaps, but still wrong.

But again, to say *that*, we would need to be able to say that some things are, in fact, bad, whether consented to or not. We would have to admit that there are some things even consenting adults shouldn't do.

Drawing Lines

Desire does not exist in a vacuum. There are kinks that fetishize inequality or that normalize oppressive preferences for race, size, or appearance. There are sexual acts that clearly eroticize degradation and dehumanization, or simply eroticize things that could harm us—on a physical or a psychic level. Some sexual preferences train us into frames of mind that could rightfully be considered unhealthy—reinforcing an expectation of instant gratification or the expectation that one should have more partners than one could ever reasonably have. In any arena other than the sexual, it would be clear that these desires reinforce oppressive structures and stereotypes, and that by breathing more life into them we are likely to make society worse for us all.

If this sounds vague, it's because so much of our behavior is contextual—and so are sexual practices. It's difficult to draw a line that works for the whole of society. But it would be good, and is in fact necessary, to ask questions about what we accept, in order to find some norm that allows *most* people to feel that their dignity is respected when they have sex.

Unfortunately, relying on consent as the only marker of what is acceptable or not has the effect of suggesting that whatever is consented to is good—"legitimization," as the scholar Robin

. puts it. It cordons off from criticism—and therefore from change!—the fairness of the social structures that motivated a particular practice, the moral standards that might allow or problematize it, and the overall goodness of the world it brings into being. It divides sex into the agreed to and the not agreed to and leaves it at that.

Objectification, Habituation, Social Degradation

So what might make a particular desire, practice, or act worthy of criticism? One clue might be objectification. The peril of objectification stems from a belief that human beings are *more* than objects, by virtue of their intrinsic dignity. To reduce them to less than that is normatively wrong: unethical.

On a concrete level, objectification often produces cognitive dissonance, a confusion of the self. It leads the objectified person to see themselves less as a person of value than an object to be manipulated, causing a variety of personal and societal harms, and accustoms the objectifier to the posture and practice of dehumanization. Its links to negative outcomes are both obvious and well studied: social science research connects the objectification of women in particular to disordered eating, appearance anxiety, body dissatisfaction, shame, depression, substance abuse, and sexual dysfunction.

More broadly, by seeing ourselves as objects (or acting as such) we deny ourselves true agency, a pose that tends to spill over into other relationships and into society at large. We may choose this objectification because it fulfills a particular desire in the short term, but it is possible for our desires to oppress us— to make it harder to see our own worth, for instance, or understand our potential or our limits. We may lean into our own subordination or degradation, for example, and find it harder than we think to lean out.

Writing in *The Guardian*, literature critic Rhiannon Lucy Cosslett mused on the prevalence of rough sex in new fiction written by women, citing stories like Kristen Roupenian's "Cat Person" and Sally Rooney's bestseller *Normal People*. "One wonders what has happened in the intervening decades that so many modern heroines seem as empty and broken as . . . pervy men want women to be. They're no longer putting up a psychological struggle. They've internalised it, they *want it*, even. That's not to say that some of this writing isn't brilliant at times, or even important; but nonetheless, I find myself craving a bit more of a fight. Instead, the reader is left feeling bleak and tawdry, as though the battle has been lost."

The battle is for the self, and the line between performance and internalization can be extremely thin. Certain sexual acts can have lasting psychological impacts; they can be an affront to our human dignity; they can also be symptomatic of issues that might be better dealt with outside of the bedroom.

ANOTHER THING TO CONSIDER when interrogating a sexual practice is what that practice does to our own character. Do the indulge make us better or worse versions of ourselves? they numb us to things that should matter or draw us away from who we would like to be? "That isn't the whole of morality, what you're doing to others," said philosopher Roger Scruton. "What you're doing to yourself is also part of morality."

Our brains habituate to things, and not always consciously, especially if sex is involved. Arousal tends to bypass critical thinking, and orgasms are a powerful reinforcement. And in the process, the images we consume can train us into desiring modes of fulfillment that make us worse individuals by any measure: more prone to prejudice and more inured to injustice, less thoughtful, less ethical, less in control of our own will. Historically, ascetic traditions have suggested that longing is important and powerful and that we should thus treat desire carefully and orient it toward the correct things. What happens when we make the choice to continually give in to the basest of our desires? Who do we become?

In season one of the hit HBO series *Girls*, Lena Dunham's character, Hannah Horvath, is having sex with her sort-of partner, Adam, when he begins to vocalize an unexpectedly offputting fantasy. Oblivious to her dismay, Adam masturbates over Hannah's chest, grinding her face into the pillow with his hand. "I . . . almost came," she says, gamely—grimly—playing along.

The scene is played for laughs; it's also pretty depressing. We intuitively find this particular sexual encounter off-putting because Adam's desire, and its expression, are for the most part overwhelmingly and alarmingly selfish and degrading. The sex is not mutual; Hannah is a (consenting, it's worth noting) prop, and she complains about it to her friends afterward.

It might be the case that this setup gets you off. It may also be worth asking why, and considering whether it is worth it to continue seeking pleasure down that road. Do you *really* want to be someone whose best experience of sex comes from degrading your partners, or being degraded by them? If a posture of total narcissism (or rag-doll acquiescence) is key to your pleasure, what effect does that have on you outside of the bedroom? It could be worth interrogating.

A further detail in that *Girls* scene: in order to climax, Adam launches into a bizarre line of dirty talk featuring Hannah as an eleven-year-old junkie with a Cabbage Patch Kids lunch box. "You're a dirty little whore," he says.

It's jarring, to say the least. It's a particularly unpleasant detail because it makes light of—indeed eroticizes—something we understand to be a great social harm: sex with children. But there are other harms less immediately awful that we can choose, or not choose, to indulge: racism, sexism, stereotypes that objectify or dehumanize, norms of subjugation based on historical harms.

We should ask whether the desires we are cultivating will actually help us flourish, make us better individually or as a society. Because our desire *is* socially mediated and it has social impacts. The desires we encourage can either improve our culture or make it worse, for ourselves and those around us.

. . .

WE TEND TO TALK of desire as though it were fixed and somehow inborn. But as feminist author Katherine Angel writes, "All sexuality is responsive; all sexual desire emerges in a culture which in turn shapes it." Our culture privileges whiteness over color and male pleasure over female, accepts gross inequality as natural and domination as exciting; above all, it sees love as a weakness. But with effort we can question, critique, and reconstruct our culture and thus our desire. And we probably should.

Sex is complicated, made more so by the various tensions imposed by biology, culture, and power. It would be ridiculous to require that all our desires remain politically correct. There is space for sex that plays with power, involves poses of domination or submission. There is space for sexual experiences that are transgressive, that pull us toward extremity with abandon. There is also space to question: Who holds the power in these encounters, and who is pretending that they do? Whose desires are preferenced, and whose are ignored? Why?

Uncritical Sex Positivity

Originally, sex positivity meant something specific. "Lust Horizons," the 1981 essay that helped coin the term, suggested that "an active, autonomous sexuality is a necessary aspect of female autonomy in general." Ellen Willis, its writer, defined being pro-sex in part as the refusal "to accept a spurious moral superiority as a substitute for sexual pleasure, and curbs on men's sexual free-dom as a substitute for real power."

This was a specific criticism aimed at a particular idea circu-lating in the feminist movement at the time, a so-called antisex view suggesting that heterosexual encounters were always tainted by gender inequality, and that political celibacy and lesbianism were the only correct responses to sex under the patriarchy. But in the same essay, Willis went on to point out that it wasn't only killjoy antisex feminists who might ruin sex. "If self-proclaimed arbiters of feminist morals stifle honest discussion with their dogmatic, guilt-mongering judgments, sexual libertarians often evade honest discussion by refusing to make judgments at all." It's a point that tends to get left behind.

Today, the term *sex positive* has ballooned in scope. Within contemporary feminism the phrase has become shorthand for a general willingness when it comes to sex—being up for any-thing, often with anyone, with an emphasis on adventurous-ness. It's "an attitude towards human sexuality that regards all consensual activities as fundamentally healthy and pleasurable and encourages sexual pleasure and experimentation," accord-ing to Flo, a women's health site. It's a way of having sex "that prioritizes personal agency and preferences and minimizes moral judgments," according to *Cosmopolitan*. "Being sex posi-tive means you get to declare, 'This is my body. This is my life. These are my desires,'" according to *Oprah Daily*. It assumes that sex is something to be traded like anything else and that any exchange can be legitimized as long as everyone consents to it. The market wants what it wants, and it's probably always right—after all, we assume that it is when it's maximizing profit in every other sphere.

This contemporary redefinition of sex positivity is cheerfully nonpolitical and appropriately capitalist, and it sidesteps the pesky question of morality; it is divorced from questions of oppression or larger social goals. Instead, it champions the primacy of appetite—our wants are above reproach and worthy of fulfillment, no matter what.

What has become difficult in our conversations about sexual norms and ethics is that they tend to run up against a principle seen as sacred in our modern politics, fueled by a discourse around individual goods and rights: while it is publicly acceptable for someone to make substantive claims about what they personally do, and how we may or may not infringe upon another person's rights, making any claims about how we should relate to each other takes on a tang of moralism and religiosity and should be negotiated in the private sphere.

But our relationships to one another are what make up our society in public *and* in private. Our actions don't take place in a vacuum, and what happens in the bedroom doesn't necessarily stay there. Perhaps we *should* talk publicly about what is good and what is not, instead of assuming that we will each sort it out correctly, alone.

There is also a difference between telling people to change their desires and inviting them to ask themselves deeper questions about them. What do we want, and who taught us to want this, and why, and how? Performing that sort of self-examination could be seen as an opportunity—to decide for oneself, to create one's sexual world rather than receiving it, labeled and performed, from a website.

The earliest sex-positive feminists were against moralizing, suspicious of checks on self-expression that posed as morality but sprang from sexual repression of the hierarchical, undeserved sort. But even they saw the risks of assuming too easily that all desire was beyond critique. In the same essay in which she coined the phrase "pro-sex feminism," Ellen Willis wrote:

> The "I'm O.K., you're O.K." brand of sexual libertarianism is a logical extension of the feminist and gay liberationist demand for the right to self-definition. But the further this principle is extended, the sharper are its contradictions. Though self-definition is the necessary starting point for any liberation movement, it can take us only so far. . . . A truly radical movement must look (to borrow a phrase from Rosalind Petchesky) beyond the right to choose, and keep focusing on the fundamental questions. Why do we choose what we choose? What would we choose if we had a real choice?

An Extreme Case

In early 2021, the actor Armie Hammer was accused of rape and abuse by two women, who leaked screenshots of alleged Instagram DMs revealing the actor's sexual fantasies about rape, torture, and, most memorably, cannibalism. ("You crying and screaming, me standing over you. I felt like such a god. I've never felt such power or intensity" was one of the tamer missives.)

Yet bizarrely, a number of established publications refused to entertain the idea that even a sexual preference that extreme might be in any way problematic. At *Slate*, an interview with a self-described "ethical cannibal" concluded that "outing someone specifically for having a fetish isn't very acceptable," describing it as "kink shaming." (The abuse allegations, in their opinion, ought to be treated as a separate issue.) "The problem is not that he has a cannibalism kink," explained Nicole Froio at Bitch Media. "It's the way he crossed boundaries again and again."

The consent violations were certainly material. But it should be obvious that the desires were, too. If someone can only get off via fantasizing about hurting their sexual partner, mutilating them and drinking their blood, isn't that at least worth a few hard questions? It should not be controversial to suggest that some of Hammer's alleged statements were normatively bad, that they perpetuate misogyny and suggest a difficulty in relating to his partners as equally valuable human beings. This is an example of a disordered, objectively vicious desire, and we should say so. Frankly, not every preference needs to be indulged.

But what was also alarming to witness was how unwilling mainstream cultural voices were to offer even the barest hint of critique. In an attempt to avoid saying anything that could be construed as moral judgment, they abdicated any claim to common sense.

IT IS WORTH IT to ask questions about what we want and why. We should question the assumption that just because we want something, or we are asked for it and consent, that the thing can be assumed to be morally neutral or even good. Hammer's example is extreme, but it is only one point along a spectrum that extends ahead and behind. It should be possible—and in fact common— to criticize sexual practices that *hurt* people in lasting ways. That betray their dignity, and whose offshoots will make for a worse culture. Yes, even if people have consented to them. Consent does not make sex physically, emotionally, or psychologically safe. An attitude of uncritical sex positivity neglects this fact.

It may be that certain sex acts are excellent for bringing us to orgasm while also putting on a pedestal some of our morally worst desires. But as a society, we should be able to point out that some states of mind are better than others, that we might want to work on satisfying certain emotions but also curbing others. A craving to dominate is generally less healthy than a desire to express affection. Jealousy is worse than love. Our individual appetites, though revealing and important, shouldn't necessarily be arbiters of what is morally good or not.

"I DON'T NEED TO THINK about the entire world when I'm having sex," is the most common pushback to the argument that social and moral considerations have a role to play in sex. "Live and let live." I would suggest, though, that we ought to think about the rest of the world more than we currently do. Our current laissez-faire ethic is based on the fiction of individual actors. But we aren't radically autonomous, as much as we'd like to think so. We are contingent particulars, shaped by those around us and shaping them. Our individual choices are linked to those of others—this is the basic nature of human society. Even if certain acts feel empowering for you in the moment, what are the social consequences?

Normalizing choking does, in fact, make it more likely that you might be surprise-choked during a sexual encounter. The rising popularity of anal sex does suggest that your teenage sibling might be pressured into it and may not know how to react. The ubiquity of pornography means that more and more women have had to deal with porn-addled men who disregard their desires or simply don't understand how to have real sex with a human being, rather than respond to an avatar on a screen.

What we champion—or just allow—will shape our broader circumstances. A society committed to a position of nonjudgment, combined with an easily fudged definition of consent, means that more people will be pushed into acts or experiences that they aren't comfortable with and will feel like they have no real grounds to push back. ("Why not? Are you *judging* me?") And as more extreme acts enter the mainstream without critique, more people will feel that they are supposed to do or want things ("It's basically *normal*, and anyway, being vanilla is boring.") that they don't truly want.

The Accelerator

Back at the holiday party, Kirsten and I stood for a few moments in uncomfortable silence. Being choked by a new partner was an experience that she clearly felt was wrong, but she wasn't sure how to critique it as such. As it turns out, surprise choking during sex isn't rare—and her discomfort wasn't unusual.

In 2019, researcher Debby Herbenick found that nearly a quarter of adult women in the U.S. reported having felt scared during sex, including a number of women who stated that their fear arose when their partners unexpectedly tried to choke them. (Additional research showed that 13 percent of sexually active girls between the ages of *fourteen and seventeen* had already experienced choking in an intimate encounter.) A BBC survey the same year found 38 percent of women to have experienced choking during consensual sex, with 42 percent reporting that they felt coerced into doing so.

Further research the next year, Herbenick told sex advice columnist Dan Savage, revealed that 21 percent of women had been choked during sex, as had 11 percent of men. "But choking during sex was much more common among 18- to 29-year-olds—almost 40 percent of whom had choked or been choked—leading us to believe that choking has really changed in the U.S., over probably the last 10 to 20 years."

Nonfatal strangulation is one of the most noticeable risk factors for future homicide, so it might seem odd that it's showing up so frequently in ostensibly positive, consensual sex. Or not, once you remember where much of our sex education is coming from: pornography.

TWO OF THE TOP TEN most visited websites in the world— and the only ones that aren't huge, branded search hubs or social media behemoths—are XVideos and Pornhub. The latter was launched only in 2007, but by 2019, Pornhub averaged 115 million visits per day, the combined equivalent of the populations of Canada, Poland, the Netherlands, and Australia.

Pornography has played a special role in turning what used to be obvious *no*s into normals, driving an uptick in acts that by the standards of even a few years ago would have been classified as extreme. Whether it's surprise choking, anal sex, polyamory, or increasingly dangerous kinks, it seems like things are on the table that simply weren't even a decade ago.

Porn is an accelerator, adding urgency to the case for thinking through the question of desire, what should be beyond critique, and what we should be able to say is good or bad.

Millennials and Gen Z are the first generations to have entered puberty accompanied by easy access to pornography via the internet—often easier access than they had to actual sex education. "I never asked a boy in my interviews *whether* he watched porn. . . . That would have shot my credibility to hell," wrote Peggy Orenstein in her 2020 bestseller *Boys & Sex*. "Because of course all of them had. Instead, my question was when they first saw it."

Smart devices and ubiquitous high-speed internet have made pornography nearly inescapable. And the most easily accessible kind is often the most depressingly amoral: aggressive and hard-core, encoded with stereotypes of race and gender, and shot from the male point of view, with women existing to give men plea-sure and not much else.

"Over time," Orenstein continued, "—and here's where this generation is unique—most of these boys learned masturbation entirely in tandem with porn, yoking it to their cycle of desire, arousal and release."

Porn has become sex ed in a real sense, a place where people learn about sex and develop their erotic imaginations. It provides models of behavior and guides expectations, and can shift sexual interests and behavior. The categories through which videos are inevitably sorted—oral, anal, ebony, blond, MILF, gangbang—mold preferences and shape desire. And porn has mainstreamed certain acts—choking, anal sex—that used to be significantly rarer; Kristen's experience and many others like it are proof.

But if porn is a form of pedagogy for so many—and it clearly is—we should question whether what it teaches is true or false, whether the preferences it champions are positive or negative, and whether what it presents is what we as a society want to be learn-ing or not. It is difficult to make the argument that the world-view it espouses has no impact on its watchers.

POPULAR PORNOGRAPHY INEVITABLY reproduces the sort of disembodiment and objectification—a penis, a hole, a neck to be

choked, a face to be abused, a body as a means to satisfaction—
that implicate it in the violence of objectification and degradation, reducing women to less than the sum of their parts and
narrowing our horizons of what sex could be.

It's also habituating. Some would say that porn is just entertainment, like a movie or a video game. But images aren't just
images; they're world making. "Life imitates art far more than
art imitates life," as Oscar Wilde wrote. In the 1970s and '80s,
feminists like Andrea Dworkin and Catharine MacKinnon posited that pornography doesn't just depict women's subordination
and violence; it trains its watchers in it and thus helps to make it
real. It was a controversial position then, but by now it seems
obviously true.

Decades of research have shown that what we consume becomes part of our psyche. When false information is inserted
into a story, people come to believe it. College students who consume porn regularly are more likely to consider the sex it por-
trays to be realistic. Men who watch porn more frequently are
less likely to empathize with rape victims and more likely to
commit sexual assault. Women who consume it report a negative effect on their identities and their relationships with men.
Exceptions exist, but it is difficult to make the argument that
pornography has been beneficial for the majority of its users.

IN AN INTERVIEW on a warm summer evening, a young man
named Zayn told me what made him finally quit watching pornography for good.

"It's an unhealthy way to satisfy a biological urge. You're having sex with, like, a machine, right? I mean, you're essentially
wiring your brain to watch a bunch of different tabs, but you
wouldn't have that many spouses or partners in the real world."
He went on: "It contributes to a weird ideal. If you get used to
seeing people like that, then you become more aware of the im-
perfections of people in real life. People don't look or act like
that, it's a kind of projection. . . . It distorts your assessment."

It made it harder, he said, for him to have relationships with
real women, even ones he would normally be attracted to, and
even one he had loved. He told me about a few years spent watching too much porn, to the point that he wasn't even excited when
in bed with a woman he felt could have been his future wife.

"I remember I had a wet dream. And the dream that I had
was like . . . I was *opening up my laptop*," he recounted. "And I
thought, 'That's weird. That's actually insane.' . . . So that's why
I stopped. That's when I was finally like, 'Oh my God, this is
terrible.' And I haven't picked it up again since January 2018.
That was the last time I watched porn."

His desire had turned mechanical, divorced from reality and
oriented toward a screen: disoriented from actual human beings.
He recognized this as a negative outcome and was right to do so.

What Could Sex Be? Who Could We Be?

He chokes me. I don't like it. But I gave consent. "Is that okay?"
At the party that December night, consent did not give me

a good response to Kirsten's tentative question. And later, I thought more about how I should have answered. At parties and over brunch, whispered at book clubs and sent in DMs by anxious college students, more and more women shared stories oddly like hers, ones where discussions of consent didn't allow the language or space to confront what else might be wrong in those situations.

We want to treat the preferences of others with respect. We should be cautious when telling others what they "really want" or what the ideal version of them "should" do—we often don't know what's right ourselves; those who convince themselves that they do are often informed less by superior knowledge and more by their own situatedness in traditions of hierarchy and power. It's also important to define sex, which cuts so clearly to the heart of the human person, in a way that is corrigible and not overly exclusionary, given how often traditions around sexuality and gender have been used to disadvantage and disempower.

Yet that doesn't mean there isn't room for ethical considerations, for a discourse that critiques our desires. Encouraging it might even be good for us. One of the best ways to make social values stick is to eroticize them: when it comes to inequality as a natural state, self-centeredness as a virtue, or contempt for women as a statement of power, this method of advocacy has worked astonishingly well. But what if we, as members of society, eroticized something else?

"The task was to liberate sex from the distortions of oppression," writes Amia Srinivasan, "not simply to divide it into the consensual (unproblematic) and non-consensual (problematic)."

Sex positivity actually had higher aims than getting private individuals off. The goal was a fairer world, radical structural change, the personal as political—not only our being free to explore our own desires but actually to free that desire from the unjust constraints that shape it.

There may not be one single answer as to what our responsibility to discipline our desire might look like. But desire shouldn't be exempt from critique.

We're not going to ban pornography—it's far too late for that. And the critiquing of desire isn't going to take place in a court. We shouldn't—and can't—call on the coercive power of the state to address all the problems of sex, because historically that sort of attempt has come at a great price. Still, it might be a positive practice to identify the substantive goods that we hope for in our encounters with each other, publicly promote practices that advance them, and publicly discourage practices that don't. The sex we choose still may not be traditional or conform to the tastes of the mainstream. But if sex has anything close to the meaning with which we've freighted it, we should want it to be more than grudgingly consented to, and more than an unthinking reflection of our most selfish impulses. And what most of us want at this point is to be moving past what we're allowed to do and toward what would be *good*.

CHAPTER 8

A New Ethic

I INTERVIEWED CARO over the phone, which was more natu-ral for her than for me. She's an audio producer, so much of her time is spent with headphones on. But even with the distance—her in Toronto, me in DC—her frank tone and dry humor made our conversations speed along. Her manner, I think, is part of what makes her work so successful. You immediately become her confidant.

For instance: "I had this experience with a guy in Denmark, and we got into, like, a philosophical debate while he was fuck-ing me in the ass."

I couldn't hold in my startled laugh.

"I met him at a bar," Caro continued, "and it was a one-night stand, and . . . I made a mistake. I was for one little moment thinking—and this was a very non-'slut pride' moment for me—I, for one tiny moment, was like, 'Is this man going to treat me worse now, because I let him fuck me in the ass before even knowing him?'"

She went on. "And then I made the double mistake of not only just *thinking* that way but then saying aloud, 'Are you going to respect me less because I'm letting you fuck me in the ass?' *While it's happening.*"

We both paused to consider the gravity of this second misstep—a truly startling break with the "don't ask, don't tell" etiquette that usually attends a one-night stand.

"So then *he* said, 'It's not . . . uh, let's not talk any more about respect. This is about lust.'" Caro stopped to draw breath then barreled on, her voice rising with every sentence. "But I said, 'I disagree. I don't think it *is* just about lust. Can we not love each other for a single day? Like, can we not treat each other with love and care and take into account your whole human person in this short period of time, which is from tonight until tomorrow morning?'"

Can we not love each other for a single day? Caro sensed— probably correctly—that her mid-ass-sex exhortation to love might be regarded as more intense than she meant it to seem, especially given the context. But she still meant it. "When I say 'love' and 'accounting for the soul,'" she later explained, "it doesn't mean that every sex act should happen within the con- fines of a committed relationship. But I do think that there should be, you know, a care that we bring to our interactions with every human on this earth and *especially* if we're fucking."

Willing the Good

When we think of "love," our minds do tend to dart toward romance: flowers, chocolate, declarations of undying devotion. But the term has a longer, richer history than just that.

Born circa 1225 in central Italy, Thomas Aquinas was a philosopher, theologian, and, eventually, one of the greatest Catholic saints. His work undergirds swaths of modern thought (what it takes for war to be just, for instance). And "willing the good of the other" was his definition of love.

Aquinas himself was borrowing that definition, not from another religious source or even a romantic tale but from another, even more foundational, philosopher: Aristotle. And in his understanding, love wasn't necessarily romantic, or even a feeling. Rather, it was an intention: to bear goodwill toward another for the sake of that person and not oneself.

There is a wide area between "consensual"—that is to say, "noncriminal"—sex and the sort of sex we want to have. This is where willing the good of the other might be the better sexual ethic we've been looking for. This sort of love entails recognizing that other people we encounter are people, like us. It asks us to reject the commodification of each other and our own sexuality, because if people are valuable, if they have intrinsic dignity, then we should not treat them as objects.

Willing someone else's good, then—the love that Caro demanded, echoing down from centuries of thinkers before her—is respect for human dignity in practice.

Aquinas was a Christian, Aristotle a pagan. The Golden Rule, or some version of it, exists in almost every society's conception of virtuous behavior: treating others as you would like to be treated in their position. Many of us no longer have a standard moral understanding, a shared conception of the common good and how to get there. This leaves us confused as to how to do right, and it's one of the reasons why we remain unsure of how to be good in our sexual relationships. But it doesn't have to be so hard.

Willing the good of the other isn't a religious concept; it's a basic suggestion for how to behave well. This ethic doesn't just apply to men; it's an equal-opportunity suggestion. And it doesn't say that sex is bad, or that you should feel bad for having it. Considering how the other person might feel and attempting to act in their best interest doesn't make flirting impossible or knock sensuality dead. It's the twenty-first century; empathy is sexy.

Willing the good means caring enough about another person to consider how your actions (and the consequences thereof) might affect them—and choosing not to act if the outcome for the other person would be negative. It's mutual concern—thinking about the experience of someone other than yourself and working to make sure that their experience is as good as you would hope yours to be. It's taking responsibility for navigating interactions that may seem ambiguous, rather than using that ambiguity as an excuse for self-serving "misunderstandings." It would ask us to will the good not generally but for our specific partners in the moment we meet them. As a practice, it might look like radical empathy: imagining ourselves in the other's stead and considering what they might feel about the encounter, not just in the moment but in the days to come.

ATTENTION TO THE OTHER is a precondition for moral attention, which is itself a precondition for empathy. And empathy is necessary for ethical action. It would mean that we have to think about the differentials in power that come with age, gender, experience, level of intoxication, and expectations of commitment, just to name a few. And it would also acknowledge that we don't know exactly what the good is, that it might—and that sex might—be something more mysterious than we imagined, that it might be different from what we currently perceive it to be. It makes it our responsibility to seek out and form an understanding of what the good actually is.

This involves a certain level of maturity and self-knowledge on our own parts: an understanding that if we aren't able to do this, in the moment or more broadly, maybe we shouldn't be having sex. Are we pursuing encounters as an outlet for emotional pain or in some other state that makes it harder for us to make thoughtful decisions? If it feels like an imposition to pause and think about another person—*your sexual partner*—that suggests a problem that lies within. This makes it less likely that we will act ethically, in which case we probably shouldn't be acting at all.

It might also mean getting to know our partners first. "When you meet someone new at a party," advises writer Leah Libresco Sargeant, "and you're both drinking, you shouldn't assume you know them well enough to tell how impaired they are by what they've drunk. It's better to wait than to hurt someone inadvertently because you didn't know them well enough to interpret their behavior."

She goes on. "There's a much bigger risk you might have sex that your partner experiences as unwanted or coerced, even if you're trying to be a good person. You just don't know each other well enough to take care of each other yet."

Often it's not just our partners' physical state we're unfamiliar with but also their emotional landscape. "If I'm thinking of willing someone else's good . . . probably I'd be more cautious about leading people on," Christopher, a teacher in his thirties, told me. "One of the most negative emotions we cause other people, especially when we're younger, is breaking each other's hearts . . . and the way we form our strongest emotional connections with people is through sex." This is also a situation in which we're better placed to act ethically if we know something about our partners: their history, their desires, their personality.

Having sex with someone who longs for more than you're willing or able to give is often cruel—it can result in corrosive feelings of rejection and of being used. But it can also be a source of deep sadness—a human emotion, but presumably one that we wouldn't wish on someone if they could be spared it. In the long run, even if this sex were consented to, it would likely hurt them. They may accept that consequence or refuse to acknowledge it, but from even a cursory understanding of the human experience, it's clear that this would be the case. If we really are looking out for our partner's good, the answer would be to refrain.

As *The Atlantic* essayist Elizabeth Bruenig has put it: "The consent question is absolutely necessary and absolutely must be answered in the affirmative for any sexual act to be ethical. . . . But so, too, should be an affirmative answer to the question 'is this good for the person?' This will bring clarity to many situations where thinking strictly in terms of consent would lead to murky or confusing results."

There are indeed many situations in which a partner might consent to sex—affirmatively, even enthusiastically—but having said sex would still be ethically wrong. In general, willing the good of the other is most often realized in restraint—in inaction, rather than action. People are far more often hurt by the sex that they have than by the sex that they fail to have. Which means that following this ethic will likely mean having less sex.

The Bureaucratic Approach

Stopping at consent is so much simpler—and purposefully so.

ATIXA 2019 was a hotel conference of the most classic, terrible kind. Outside in Philadelphia it was a sunny seventy-nine degrees, but inside the Association of Title IX Administrators East Coast Annual Conference, the temperature hovered around a bone-chilling sixty-two. The host hotel featured the type of industrial air-conditioning that forced conference-goers to wear puffer jackets indoors, as well as grim fluorescent lighting that defied the sun's existence. The ballroom where the main panels took place had a murky brown carpet with mysterious spiral designs, while the stage and podium were draped in an ill-fitting burgundy polyester swag.

"Do I have to wear a name tag? I'm just observing." I asked at the check-in table, having arrived late on day one and already feeling oppressed by the cold. "Yep!" chirped the bored attendant. My tag had a bright blue ribbon that proclaimed me a FIRST TIME ATTENDEE in big gold letters. Apparently, some people had to go to this every year.

Make that most, not just some. The majority of attendees were in town less for the informational panels like "The Current State of Sexual Harassment" (still bad, one might assume?) than for the sort of expensive certification courses that have made sexual assault trainings a booming business for collegiate administrative consultancy firms. These courses were where college bureaucrats learned the correct terms for various degrees of sexual misconduct along with the correct guardrails to protect their students from assault—and, perhaps more importantly, to protect themselves from legal action, reputational risk, or the withdrawal of federal funding.

Repeated over and over again was the word *consent*, touted as a cure-all for an unhealthy campus sexual culture. "Consent is clear, knowing, voluntary (or affirmative, conscious and voluntary) words and actions that give permission for specific sexual activity," according to the ATIXA "Investigation in a Box" tool kit ("EVERYTHING YOU NEED TO PROFESSIONALIZE YOUR CAMPUS CIVIL RIGHTS INVESTIGATIONS," it advertises). For an overworked Title IX administrator seeking a bright line for what counts as sexual misconduct—and specifically, the kind of misconduct for which he or she could be held liable for not addressing—consent is highlighter yellow. When it's present, whatever "sexual contact" that might have happened is not your harried functionary's concern. When it's not, you have a problem on your hands. Luckily, the absence of consent should resolve the case for you—the instigating party is guilty, and peace prevails. Until it doesn't.

But whatever the failings of an ethical system created by an ass-covering university bureaucracy, it does have one thing going for it: fear. In 2014, the state of California passed a bill requiring public universities to adopt affirmative consent standards in their adjudication of sexual assault. Going forward, rape would be defined by the absence of an affirmative consent from the alleged victim rather than by the presence of nonconsent, meaning that if it wasn't made completely clear that both parties consented to a sexual encounter, the college could find that the person who didn't consent was assaulted. It made it possible to criminalize a whole swath of sexual encounters in which the agreement to proceed had remained unspoken.

Then–*Vox* columnist Ezra Klein wrote that it was a terrible bill but that he completely supported it. "The Yes Means Yes law is a necessarily extreme solution to an extreme problem. Its overreach is precisely its value."

He went on: "It will settle like a cold winter on college campuses, throwing everyday sexual practice into doubt and creating a haze of fear and confusion over what counts as consent. This is the case against it, and also the case for it. Because for one in five women to report an attempted or completed sexual assault means that everyday sexual practices on college campuses need to be upended, and men need to feel a cold spike of fear when they begin a sexual encounter."

There is something to be said for this sort of fear. Perhaps men *should* be nervous, so nervous that they make an analysis of their actions in the same way women do—and not just an analysis of their actions but an analysis of what their partner might think, what the other person might feel. Yet even this stricter, more punitive version of consent doesn't solve the deeper problems of our sexual culture and creates others, too.

For instance: while women tend to be more at risk in sexual situations by virtue of physical power dynamics, men can get hurt, too. False rape accusations are rare, but even a quickly resolved investigation can derail a college career, and a life, for years afterward. Not every sexual misstep is a crime, but we tend to punish them as though they were, ignoring the fact that our rules are so impoverished that they are easy to misconstrue. Plus, as is the case with everything else in our criminal justice system, we end up levying the harshest punishment against the poorest, darkest, or otherwise most undefended of those accused . . . but not necessarily those most in the wrong.

The law combats crime not by eliminating criminality but by increasing the risk attached to it; a stronger and more legible moral ideal might combat crimes by creating people who have no plans to commit them in the first place. What we need is a better framework, some sort of context for what people should and should not be doing, for what will be deemed acceptable and what will not. And this is where we have to move from laws to ethics—from banal rule following to a higher aspiration. And at the heart of any ethic is a concern about someone other than ourselves, something other than our own desires and our own self-interest.

The question shouldn't just be "Did I avoid raping this person?"—that's the floor, not the ceiling. The question should be "Did I do something good here—not just for myself but for my partner? Did we"—because sex between two people should be concerned with more than just one of them—"treat each other well?" Asking "Do I have permission?" is very different from asking "How does this make you feel?" The former question is a checkbox. The latter implies a continuing responsibility for our actions. Willing the good of the other is a positive stance: connecting with our partners in a manner that is cooperative rather than antagonistic.

IF YOU LOOK CLOSELY, you can see similarities in some of the scenarios women have spoken out against—the Cat Persons, the babe.nets, the multitude of dates and hangouts that have resulted in unwanted sex or even just lingering emotional pain.

And it's clear that the one thing that all of those have in common is that the offender was *self-centered*: they were overvaluing their own preferences, refusing to take responsibility for their partner's good.

A new and better sexual ethic moves our goals away from the individual and the negative—"not getting Me Too'd," or even "not being sad after sexual encounters"—toward the collaborative and the positive: "Am I present to the needs of my partner? Is this good for the other person? How do I behave humanely toward others?" It demands *paying attention*, as a necessary precondition for ethical behavior.

Some might say that this mindset is paternalistic. How dare you ask me to decide for someone else? How could you tell someone to decide for me? But what this ethic actually asks for is awareness, not overreach.

I asked Grace, a brash, fast-talking twenty-three-year-old whose college sexual assault had made headlines at her Ivy League school, what a good sexual world would look like.

"I have a hard time imagining the ideal . . . but I guess what that looks like is listening. Very intentional listening and presence. Because I think it's really hard to hurt somebody if you're present with them."

The lessons at ATIXA were about listening, in the most limited sense: listening for the consent code words that would clear someone from responsibility in a sexual encounter. They weren't about the sort of listening, the sort of care, that women like Grace and Caro wished for, and that many of their peers did as well.

"I think bad sexual encounters happen because one person has an end goal that isn't mutual," Grace continued. "If the end goal is sex, and not sex *with* someone, if that makes sense. I think that the good sexual encounter has to have both people fully there."

She laughed, then sighed. "That was more poetry bullshit than it was a tangible answer."

It wasn't. She was right.

CHAPTER 9

Rethinking Sex

IN THE MID-2010S, the much-loved and now-defunct website *The Hairpin* published a series of interviews with adult virgins. The framing was clear enough—virgins, apparently, were so rare and strange that they needed to be discovered, interviewed, and cataloged as though they were members of an uncontacted Amazonian tribe. But the interviews were even more revealing.

Said Maya, a twenty-six-year-old med student in DC: "[Virginity] is a strange and really powerful burden to have to feel, as a young woman who embraces contemporary life and culture. I don't feel like I'm an antiquated thinker. I respect and value everything that's changed in this world for women. Yet if I told most people that I believed in keeping my virginity for my husband, they'd almost instantly see me as a Bible-beating Victorian."

Said Ben, a twenty-six-year-old master's student in New York City: "I don't want to end up in the same boat twenty years from now. I know that being a virgin is a liability which will only increase over time. Women don't want to deal with a neophyte."

Said Bette, a thirty-two-year-old London financier: "Not having erotic capital, not being part of the sexual marketplace . . . that's a serious thing in our world! I mean, practically everyone has sex, so what's wrong with me?"

All of these sentiments resonated with me and my own experience of being what I jokingly described to close friends as a "late-stage virgin." I too had had the feeling that I was missing out, stunting my own development, making my own life harder. But in the long run, was I?

"I do feel like there is this like shame around people who don't have sex," one woman told me. "I'm guilty of this. A friend will tell me she hasn't had sex in two years and I'll be like, 'You have to get yourself out there! You're just wasting time!' . . . But also, is that really going to be the best use of her time? She's probably better off doing what she enjoys, and casual sex isn't one of those things. Who cares?"

What If We Had Less Sex?

The freedom of the sexual revolution seems to go in only one direction. We are certainly free to have sex in the manner in which we choose (although for women, the Madonna/whore construct and other forms of judgment still loom), but *not* having sex is a stigmatized choice. No one will force you to do it (hopefully), but you should at least want to, preferably as soon as possible. If having sex was once taboo, *not* having it is today. After all, who wants to be a low-capital, neophyte, Victorian liability?

In her book *The Sex Myth*, Rachel Hills described why the ongoing cultural obsession with sex—which quickly shades into a personal one—actually does harm to women and men. It defines "not only what we *cannot* do without fear of stigma or harm, but what we feel we *must* do in order to avoid feelings of shame and inadequacy." The project of sex positivity is meant to increase our sense of independence and empowerment, but being pressured into a single understanding of what you must and must not do is the literal opposite of personal freedom.

Still, there is a weird horror at the suggestion that we accept having less sex than we currently do. In fact, one of the most pernicious stories we tell ourselves is one about our desperate need for sexual fulfillment and the overweening power of desire.

In 2017, near the peak of the #MeToo movement, journalist Masha Gessen penned a column in *The New Yorker* under the headline "When Does a Watershed Become a Sex Panic?" In an attempt to caution women against going too far with their revelations, Gessen wrote in solemn yet horrified tones: "The policing of sex seems to assume that it's better to have ten times less sex than to risk having a nonconsensual sexual experience."

"Policing" implies something negative, an intrusion, one

that may end in an innocent person's death. Is it really "policing" sex to name one's experiences and point out that some actions are not good, at best, and perhaps even criminal?

And then there is "seems to assume," suggesting that this statement is not, in fact, something we have agreed upon. So what are we undecided about? Do we no longer agree that, when weighing the things that we value, maintaining a human person's dignity and bodily autonomy is more important than having "ten times" more sex?

In the end, the headline gave it away. This mindset is not one of sex positivity; this *is* sex panic, but from the supposedly liberated side. It's a sexual philosophy of fear: fear that if we are asked to reconsider the ways we have and talk about sex, a tyrant might appear and tell us that we can't have any at all.

IN THE CONTEMPORARY ERA, we have become accustomed to treating our desires as something to be satisfied as immediately as possible—eat the cake, buy the shoes, have the sex—otherwise we risk the charge of not being true to ourselves. We describe sex in particular as a need, hearkening back to our Freudian (and liberal-capitalist) understandings of deprivation as a fate worse than death. Sexual desire is an uncontrollable force, stronger than any norms, customs, responsibilities, or relationships that might stand in its way, and it's often too much to ask for us to control ourselves in the face of it.

But it's possible that we are actually overselling sex, and underselling our own free will.

Sex is an important part of the human experience: an intense form of pleasure, a biological urge that it's perfectly okay—natural, even—to want. But viewing it as *just* that is misleading. For all that sex is a deep-set urge, we are still human beings, rational creatures who can, in fact, transcend our biology. Framing sex as a categorical imperative—"must have it, or else"—is what allows predators to justify sexual harassment and assault as what they need to do in order to get off. And though controlling ourselves might not be as pleasurable in the moment, we aren't actually animals. We do have the ability to think in the long term and pick logic over momentary feelings and thoughts. In fact, we have a responsibility—to ourselves and to others—to do so.

As sex educator Emily Nagoski has often pointed out, nobody has ever died of sexlessness: "We can starve to death, die of dehydration, even die of sleep deprivation. But nobody ever died of not being able to get laid."

And the push to have ever more sex—especially casual sex—has not necessarily resulted in more satisfaction. "This great sex experience that the market commands every optimised self-managed subject to be consuming isn't good sex," critic Sophie Lewis writes. "Porn is now precisely taxonomized and accessible, hooking up is algorithmically managed, being 'horny on main' has gained acceptability, yet desire seems elusive."

Americans who have many sexual partners don't appear to be happier than their more prudish counterparts, according to a 2019 analysis of sexual behavior by sociologist Nick Wolfinger. In fact, there is an inverse correlation between sexual promiscuity and success in long-term relationships, which, more than a

wildly experimental sex life, is what the majority of adults profess to want. By focusing only on our most obvious appetites, we
may be ignoring our deeper and more lasting desires.

"Would my life be the same?" Brooke had asked after our
conversation about her rape and everything that came after. "Or
maybe even better, if all of the terrible hookups never happened?
Probably." She paused. "So, like, I think . . . I should just stop
adding more of them."

What if the answer is less, not more?

The Pause

Brooke wasn't the only one thinking along these lines.

On a freezing-cold Sunday morning in January, I caught up
with some college students at a noisy brunch spot on the Upper
West Side. The three juniors and I were squeezed in tightly
around a table, but the volume of sound around us—combined
with my companions' habit of finishing each other's sentences—
meant that I had to beg them to lean in around my tape re-
corder. As our voices rose and fell, and terms like *blow jobs*, *hookup*,
and *venereal disease* cut through the din, the staid, sweater-over-
button-down crowd around us raised their eyebrows while pretending not to listen in. These well-mannered youths could be
their own children, after all, out on winter break.

Vivian, a twenty-one-year-old French major who had grown
up in England, described a hookup in which her partner had said

he didn't want to have sex, to the amazement of the friends she told about it afterward. "We were taken aback that there was someone with the opportunity to potentially have sex who would refrain from it to prioritize . . . getting to know someone?" She still sounded faintly amazed. "It was really nice, but that shouldn't be so—" Her friend AJ, a bright-eyed econ major from New York, cut in. "We shouldn't have to treat it like he's a unicorn."

"We were literally like, 'Oh my God,'" Vivian said, widening her eyes to demonstrate their surprise "'He's such a good guy.' But it shouldn't be that crazy."

Do you want that, though? I asked. To wait, to get to know someone before sleeping with them?

"In retrospect? I think it's really nice." She repeated herself more quietly. "It was really nice."

Autumn, a twenty-year-old history major who still retained her prep-school vocal tics, chimed in. "I think I would want that. In retrospect there are, like, lots of situations that I've been in that were not worth it. That did more damage than they did good."

At this point, both Vivian and AJ were nodding along.

"You do it because, like . . . that's what people think sex is. But if it was about more than just them getting off, like, actually wanting things to be good for the other person . . . I think in some ways that can only come about either if you're a really, *really* nice person, or you actually care about the other person."

"Yeah." She smiled. "So maybe people should stop hooking up until they love each other."

THE IDEA SEEMED almost shocking to those college students, but it was something I had heard proposed with increasing frequency the more people I spoke to. What if the answer was to have less casual sex? For that matter, what if the answer was to have sex under the standard of love?

In a 2015 interview, Dan Savage was asked if there were any issues on which he, as a long-tenured and famously open-minded sex columnist, had changed his mind.

"When I started my column it was 1991 . . . the party line was that it didn't matter how many people you'd had sex with, it mattered how. If you were having safe sex and using condoms, you could have sex with a million people, and that was just as safe as having unsafe sex with one person."

It turned out that for him, the baseline he advocated has changed. "I don't believe that anymore," he continued. "With my life experience, with the experience of my friends, even reading letters for the column, I'd say it does seem to matter how many people you've had sex with. The more people you're crawling into bed with, the higher the chance you're crawling into bed with someone who doesn't care about you."

Just a few years later, in a newly callous era of dating apps and sensitized by the #MeToo movement, more and more people were looking for care—to be seen, and be treated as if they, and sex, *mattered*. And it was becoming increasingly clear that to make that plausible, a drop in sexual volume was essential.

Much of the discussion so far has been framed from the female point of view. And that's fair, because it's women who have by far gotten the short end of the stick. They're more likely to be assaulted, less likely to derive pleasure from these sexual encounters, and more likely to be either ignored or criticized (or, almost miraculously, some combination of both!) when they complain. Ideally, the responsibility to carry out this new ethic would fall equally on men and women. But in reality, it will be women for whom it feels most urgent.

But men also have much to gain.

If too many women feel pressure to say yes, too many men feel the pressure not to say no. And the presumption that men are always looking for sex makes it harder for them to speak about being sexually assaulted or coerced. It encourages emotional repression and the trivialization of real feeling and care. It makes it even harder for men to admit that what they actually might want is a real relationship rather than casual sex. Men are more than just mindless sex havers, objectifying women and pursuing their physical needs after getting perfunctory consent. The lies that men tell—or have been told—about themselves are harmful too.

IN THE SUMMER OF 2020, one of my friends told me about a new venture: Project Celibacy.

182 — RETHINKING SEX

At first, contra everything that I have written so far, I laughed. It didn't seem like him; his sex life was notoriously active. "Can you define Project Celibacy for me?" I asked.

He blushed. "It's not having—not having sex for . . . at least a month. Or not having sex except with people with whom there is a path to a long-term relationship. So I *could* break it, but only for the right reasons."

"Why?"

"I want to make decisions about really important things. But that means a complete reorientation of the way I think about sex."

THE STOIC EPICTETUS wrote to his students: "When you receive an invitation to pleasure . . . pause." We need to reclaim this pause.

To those of us brought up in the wake of the sexual revolution, this might sound like a call for repression. But it doesn't have to be a rejection of our sexuality or desire. On the contrary, it can be more freeing—and agency giving—to be able to say no, especially in a culture that pushes us to say yes to everything, whether we want to or not. When it's assumed that you'll do something, *not* doing it can be the more personal choice. And embracing those old values—prudence, temperance, even *chastity*, might give us the space to stop and think, and to decide what we don't want and make room for what we do.

In her book *Chastened*, London book critic Hephzibah Anderson wrote about choosing to embark on a self-imposed year of no sex, after realizing that she wanted to take more control over her emotional life after a decade of dead-end relationships, and quit the habit of sleeping with partners just because it seemed like the done thing. She acknowledged that talking about her decision felt taboo—"bizarrely, when it's assumed that you will sleep with someone, not sleeping with them can become a more personal choice"—but she also found the experience clarifying.

"There were moments of intense physical longing during my chaste year, but I also realised that some of that longing wasn't really for sex. . . . I remembered that romance was a verb, and learned to savour forgotten emotions like yearning. I also realised how some regrets—not sleeping with a guy, as opposed to sleeping with him, for instance—could be almost sweet." Anderson noticed that she was drawn to different kinds of partners, and that delaying physical intimacy often gave her more space to open up emotionally. It was a challenge, she said, but ultimately a liberating one.

"My instinct tells me that we should treat sex like we should treat anything pleasurable," says writer Katherine Dee. "Sometimes, the joy will come from thrilling circumstances, or that we're doing something naughty. But that's a quick jolt, a sugar rush, and ultimately not sustainable. For joy to be sustainable, it has to be earned."

This is an argument for restraint. In every other situation common to the human experience—eating, drinking, exercise, even email—we have realized that restraint produces healthier results. Why not here, too? Having lots of sex hasn't led to better sex or better relationships. In many cases, it has inspired numbness, callousness, hurting others and being hurt. And rather than being titillating, sexual overload is *boring*. Boundaries can make things more exciting, more beautiful, paradoxically *more* open to the possibility of something better and as yet unimagined.

Change

I should admit that it took me a while to arrive here myself.

Coming of age in Virginia in the midnineties, when the abstinence-only sex education movement was in full swing, we didn't really talk about sex. At my public middle school, there were the requisite gender-segregated assemblies where the girls learned about our growing chests, our sprouting hair, and our periods, and received Tampax-sponsored samples of pads and tampons. (What did the boys learn? To this day, I'm not entirely sure.) I was left to glean further information from the romance novels I paged through secretively in the library (often the pages of the good bits had already been bent by previous seekers).

In high school, "The Reproductive System" was just another section in our battered health textbooks. Memorize diagrams of the urethra, uterus, and fallopian tubes? No problem. Actually talk about what having sex meant? No thanks. I was never even taught how to put on a condom (again, thank you, abstinence-only education), though my health class did watch an ancient, alarming VHS tape featuring close-ups of various advanced-stage STIs.

The gaps in my knowledge weren't filled outside of school, either. I grew up evangelical—for as long as I can remember, my family went to church on Sundays, sometimes twice—a cornerstone of our relationship with a loving but rather judgmental God. I was steeped in a culture of Wednesday-night youth group and overnight "lock-ins" in which girls and guys slept on different sides of the gym and our earnest youth leaders gave us vague advice about guarding our hearts and resisting temptation.

I escaped the worst of purity culture (sex-havers as chewed gum, licked Oreos, or worse), but still absorbed some key messages: Sex was something serious. Therefore, staying abstinent would keep me from being hurt or damaged.

And then I went to college, where the expectation was that incoming students already knew everything that we needed, and also, apparently, that everyone would be having sex all the time. The only rule was "consent," and we saw it as our duty to keep our emotions in check in the name of preserving our freedom: freshman girls training to become perfect partners for twenty-one-year-old guys who wanted to have sex and move on.

I held on to my abstinence for a while and then let it go, jumping into the opposite end of the pool. I found that neither extreme made sense. Total openness wasn't actually more freeing than the cramped confines of purity culture. I watched my peers get hurt; I got hurt too. But some lessons from that culture—where salvageable—still had value, I realized over time. Sex wasn't everything, but it meant *something*. And it was best with someone who cared—and not everyone who wanted to have sex with me would. This was the deep-rooted understanding that, when I listened to it, consistently made sense.

My own mindset had ping-ponged a bit, from purity culture to a rebellion against it to something in between. But I finally . . . stopped. Not stopped dating or even became celibate—or at least, not on purpose. But I did press pause. What did I want out of sex? Out of my relationships? If I was honest with myself, neither total abstinence nor assimilation to mainstream sexual culture would help me obtain the connection I truly desired, and neither coincided with my sense of self.

In my most recent relationships, I've taken some time before having sex. That decision is made not out of repression or fear: it's because I think that sex is meaningful, and I want to treat it as such—to live in alignment with what I believe. I don't owe anyone access to my body. I don't have anything to prove. If there's something there in a potential relationship, it will still be there—and may even grow clearer, more defined, for waiting. So far, this assumption has held true.

SEXUAL PLEASURE DIDN'T begin with the sexual revolution. And loving relationships aren't synonymous with virginity and marriage. Less casual sex doesn't have to equal no sex until marriage—that train left the station a long time ago. But creating a better sexual culture and a healthier sexuality would probably mean recognizing sex as something unique—powerful, personal, intimate—that should be respected and handled with care.

We're in an era of extremes. What we need is a healthier sexual ethic, if only to find a balance that will serve us well. That will take telling the truth about sex: its emotionality, its biology, the societal factors that influence us. It will also mean balancing our desires with our responsibility to others, and recognizing that consent is not enough. And it will take community, not to shame or stigmatize but to engage in a continual reform, rather than relying on reductive rules.

IN 2019 *The New York Times* published an article on secular millennials who had gone to live with nuns—not in order to become religious but to figure out how to live lives in line with their own radical, progressive values. They found that old wisdoms can still feed change, and that restraint didn't need to mean a closing down—it could also mean an opening up.

"I started to realize chastity was an invitation to 'right relationship' and not just about celibacy," said one, Sarah Jane Bradley. "In an era of Me Too, we need right relationships. We need to know what it means to respect someone's personhood and to respect your own personhood and to be a conduit for love rather than ego needs."

If anything, more restraint might give us more freedom to seek and offer love.

AT MY BRUNCH with the college students, Autumn remarked: "I have very high expectations for all of my friends and the people they have sex with, and I think that some things definitely shouldn't be tolerated. But then I very much turn around and do the exact opposite." In this, she reminded me very much of myself.

This is an uncomfortable chapter to write—an uncomfortable *book* to write. It's difficult to propose that anyone change their ways without also pointing a finger at oneself. It will always be easier to justify how what *I* am doing is right, or at least right enough.

Being able to identify failures is key to creating a new norm. But one way to move forward—to put that norm into practice rather than be stymied by its seeming unattainability—is to simply be open to recalibration. To not be defined by our past experiences and to choose better once we know how. Condemning what we see as bad is fine, of course. But we should devote even more energy to finding something we can see as good.

Disappointment shouldn't be our default state. Happiness shouldn't feel as though it's out of reach. If you've gotten all the way here, I hope you now feel a little less alone in being not okay with the state of our sexual culture. It's not crazy to want something more. It's perfectly reasonable to ask for better than we have—and something better may really be possible.

We were made for connection—in truth, we were made for love. And knowing this, we should feel confident that ethical, pleasurable, caring sexual encounters are truly possible, *and* that our wholeness and humanity doesn't depend on our having sex at all. Reshaping the culture will take work, of course: imagination and empathy and conversation and critique. But the project of cultivating our own ethics, morality, and humanity is worth it, even if nothing else changes.

The shift might feel uncomfortable at first: awkward, or extreme. But we can get there. And by rethinking sex, we can make it better for us all.

Acknowledgments

Thank you to my agent, Gary Morris, who understood this project when it was merely the germ of an idea and shepherded it into the best hands.

Thank you to Bria Sandford, an excellent editor and an excellent friend, who believed that I could take this topic on and steered me deftly through the highs and lows of a first book. Apologies again for all the late-night texts.

Thank you to Nina Rodriguez-Marty, Mary Kate Skehan, Amanda Lang, Pamela Peterson, and the rest of the Penguin team for ushering this book into world with great spirit, and for lending some to me.

Thank you to Fred Hiatt, who gave me space to write and believed that I'd make it back: your trust gave me confidence.

Thank you to the entire *Washington Post* Opinions section for the cheerful advice and encouragement, and the expressions of surprise, delight, and concern each time I resurfaced in the office after being MIA for months.

Thank you to the FGs: Reilly Kiernan, Molly Alarcon, Mary Marshall, Jess Lanney. You've let me test out my theories, you've sharpened my ideas, and you've made me a more compassionate thinker—in this book and in life. Friendship is truly the best ship.

Thank you to Samuel Kimbriel, for the long walks and deep talks, and Leah Libresco, whose feedback was invaluable.

Thank you to my family: Mom, Dad, Christopher, Cheta, and Faith (who finally gets to be an early reader)—I'm nothing without your support.

Thank you to all of the women and men who told me their stories, for letting me into your lives and helping us all feel less alone. I hope you feel the same.

Thank you to the experts who shared their wisdom, insight, and time.

Thank you to Boris, who filled my book leaves with adventure and introduced me to a different way of living.

Thank you to Josh, for your good cheer, tough edits, and constant reassurance. I promise I'll go to sleep someday.

Deo Gratias, I'm so grateful.

Notes

Chapter 1: Solving the Wrong Problem

4 **"Throughout my high school"**: Rebecca Alifimoff, "How Aziz Ansari Made Me Rethink Rape Culture at Penn," *Daily Pennsylvanian*, January 24, 2018, https://www.thedp.com/article/2018/01/rebecca-alifimoff-aziz-ansari -upenn-penn-rape-culture-sexual-assault.

7 **"'You don't get to have sex'"**: Amia Srinivasan, "Does Anyone Have the Right to Sex?" *London Review of Books*, March 22, 2018, https://www.lrb.co .uk/the-paper/v40/n06/amia-srinivasan/does-anyone-have-the-right-to-sex.

8 **"Sexual liberals have promoted"**: Ellen Willis, "Toward a Feminist Sexual Revolution," *Social Text*, no. 6 (Autumn 1982): 3–21, https://doi.org/10 .2307/466614.

9 **babies in neonatal intensive**: Katharina Rowold, "What Do Babies Need to Thrive? Changing Interpretations of 'Hospitalism' in an International Context, 1900–1945," *Social History of Medicine* 32, no. 4 (2019): 799–818.

12 **in twelve European countries**: Louise Osborn, "Denmark: Reform Recognizes Sex Without Consent as Rape," *Deutsche Welle*, December 17, 2020, https://www.dw.com/en/denmark-reform-recognizes-sex-without-consent -as-rape/a-55971758.

12 **The entire concept was ridiculed:** "Is It Date Rape?" *Saturday Night Live*, season 19, episode 2, directed by Dave Wilson, written by James Downey, Tony de Sena, and Dave Attell, aired October 2, 1993, on NBC.

12 **Dave Chappelle was still roasting the idea:** "Love Contract," *Chappelle's Show*, season 2, episode 4, directed by Rusty Cundieff, written by Neal Brennan and Dave Chappelle, aired February 11, 2004, on Comedy Central.

12 **in five U.S. states:** California, New York, Colorado, Connecticut, and Illinois now require public colleges and universities to apply affirmative consent guidelines in adjudicating campus sexual assault, even though the states' criminal statutes define sexual assault more narrowly.

12 **you change their diaper:** Britni de la Cretaz, "How to Start Teaching Your Kids About Consent Even When They're a Baby," *Romper*, November 9, 2015, www.romper.com/p/how-to-start-teaching-your-kids-about-consent-even -when-theyre-a-baby-306

13 **"living in her father's house":** Brooke Flagler, "A Brief History of Rape Law," The Feminist Poetry Movement, December 13, 2019, https://sites .williams.edu/engl113-f18/flagler/a-brief-history-of-rape-law/.

14 **tiny liberal arts school:** Samantha Stark, "'I Kept Thinking of Antioch': Long Before #MeToo, a *Times* Video Journalist Remembered a Form She Signed in 2004," *New York Times*, April 8, 2018, https://www.nytimes.com /2018/04/08/insider/antioch-sexual-consent-form-metoo-video.html.

Chapter 2: We're Liberated, and We're Miserable

22 **"The share of Americans":** Kate Julian, "Why Are Young People Having So Little Sex?" *Atlantic*, December 2018, www.theatlantic.com/magazine /archive/2018/12/the-sex-recession/573949/.

24 **"Ban Men" cross-stitch:** Amanda Hess, "The Rise of the Ironic Man-Hater," *Slate*, August 8, 2014, https://slate.com/human-interest/2014/08 /ironic-misandry-why-feminists-joke-about-drinking-male-tears-and -banning-all-men.amp.

24 **"usually expressed in the form":** Indiana Seresin, "On Heteropessimism," *New Inquiry*, October 9, 2019, https://thenewinquiry.com/on-hetero pessimism/.

25 **"Nearly everything I know":** Dolly Alderton, *Everything I Know About Love* (New York: HarperCollins, 2020), 314, 358.

27 **"[As lesbian separatists] we believe":** Jackie Anderson, "Separatism, Feminism, and the Betrayal of Reform," *Signs* 19, no. 2 (1994): 437–48, http:// www.jstor.org/stable/3174806.

28 **interested in dating *them*:** Anna Brown, "Nearly Half of U.S. Adults Say Dating Has Gotten Harder for Most People in the Last 10 Years," Pew Re-

search Center, August 20, 2020, www.pewresearch.org/social-trends/2020
/08/20/nearly-half-of-u-s-adults-say-dating-has-gotten-harder-for-most
-people-in-the-last-10-years/#fnref-28925-1.

30 **"I don't think older generations":** roobz (@tishray), Twitter, April 1,
2021, 4:21 p.m., https://twitter.com/tishray/status/1377763117233549317
?lang=en.

30 **Fully half of single:** Brown, "Nearly Half of U.S. Adults."

30 **a fourteen-point increase:** Wendy Wang, "The Share of Never Married
Americans Has Reached a New High," *Institute for Family Studies*, September 9, 2020, https://ifstudies.org/blog/the-share-of-never-married-americans
-has-reached-a-new-high.

30 **thirteen percentage points in thirteen years:** Mark Regnerus, *Cheap Sex:
The Transformation of Men, Marriage, and Monogamy* (New York: Oxford
University Press, 2017), 32.

31 **adults may never marry:** Wendy Wang and Kim Parker, "Record Share of
Americans Have Never Married," Pew Research Center, September 24, 2014,
www.pewresearch.org/social-trends/2014/09/24/record-share-of-americans
-have-never-married/.

31 **constitute sexual harassment:** "Over-Friendly, or Sexual Harassment? It
Depends Partly on Whom You Ask," *Economist*, November 17, 2017, https://
www.economist.com/graphic-detail/2017/11/17/over-friendly-or-sexual
-harassment-it-depends-partly-on-whom-you-ask.

32 **"One of the most important pleasures":** Fannie Bialek, in discussion with
the author, December 13, 2019.

34 **"The renewed interest in Dworkin":** Michelle Goldberg, "Not the Fun
Kind of Feminist," *New York Times*, February 22, 2019, www.nytimes.com
/2019/02/22/opinion/sunday/trump-feminism-andrea-dworkin.html.

38 **"The larger reimagining of sexual pleasure":** Ariel Levy, *Female Chau-
vinist Pigs* (New York: Simon & Schuster, 2006), 55.

38 **"gentle, tender people":** Germaine Greer, *The Female Eunuch* (London:
Paladin, 1970).

39 **"mixing up cocktails":** Hugh Hefner, *Playboy*, December 1953.

40 **"end of Puritanism":** Gay Talese, *Thy Neighbor's Wife* (Garden City, NY:
Doubleday, 1980), 106.

40 **bestselling book *Sex and the Single Girl*:** Helen Gurley Brown, *Sex and the
Single Girl* (New York: Bernard Geis, 1962).

40 **"girl of our times":** Gurley Brown, *Sex and the Single Girl*.

40 **"sexually zonk him":** Helen Gurley Brown, *Having It All: Love, Success,
Sex, Money Even If You're Starting with Nothing* (New York: Simon & Schuster, 1982).

41 **"devout feminist":** Helen Gurley Brown, Interview, CNN, 1996, https://
www.cnn.com/videos/us/2012/08/13/bts-helen-gurley-brown-feminist.cnn.

43 **"is centrally predicated on commanding":** Sophie Lewis, "Collective Turn-off," *Mal Journal*, July 2020, https://maljournal.com/5/sex-negative /sophie-lewis/collective-turn-off/.

44 **"To a surprising degree":** Hanna Rosin, "Boys on the Side," *Atlantic*, September 2012, www.theatlantic.com/magazine/archive/2012/09/boys-on-the -side/309062/.

45 **"becomes a smokescreen for the strong":** Jo Freeman, "The Tyranny of Structurelessness," *Ms.*, July 1973, 76–78 and 86–89.

46 **"[sexual revolution] propaganda has undermined":** Ellen Willis, "Up from Radicalism: A Feminist Journal, Revisited," originally published in 1969, republished by *Guernica*, May 1, 2014, www.guernicamag.com/up-from -radicalism.

Chapter 3: We Want to Catch Feelings

50 **"The zipless fuck is absolutely pure":** Erica Jong, *Fear of Flying* (New York: Holt, Rinehart and Winston, 1973), Kindle location 398.

53 **"one of the biggest feminist movements":** Nina Bradley, "These Quotes from 'Sex and the City' Are Still So Relatable," *Bustle*, October 26, 2017, www.bustle.com/p/19-quotes-from-sex-the-city-that-are-still-amazing-13 -years-later-2909300.

54 **One article in *New York* magazine's blog:** Lydia Kiesling, "I Met My Husband When I Was 22 and Wild," *The Cut*, December 18, 2019, www.thecut .com/2019/12/i-met-my-husband-when-i-was-22-and-wild.html.

55 **"I'm in my twenties":** Kaitlin Prest and WNYC Studios, "In the No Part 1," *Radiolab*, October 11, 2018, https://www.wnycstudios.org/podcasts/radiolab /articles/no-part-1.

57 **"I think it's a fallacy":** Lori Gottlieb in discussion with the author, August 11, 2020.

60 **"Chill has now slithered":** Alana Massey, "Against Chill," *Matter*, April 1, 2015, https://medium.com/matter/against-chill-930dfb60a577.

61 **"After throwing ourselves into":** Charlotte Shane, "Swipe Right on Monogamy," Posts from the Near Future, *Matter*, December 23, 2015, https:// medium.com/matter/swipe-right-on-monogamy-189b55568c0c.

62 **"The [1984] Nightmare":** Shulamith Firestone, *The Dialectic of Sex: The Case for Feminist Revolution* (New York: William Morrow and Company, 1970).

Chapter 4: Men and Women Are Not the Same

69 **"Modern woman is at last":** "The FDA Approves the Pill," American Experience, PBS.org, www.pbs.org/wgbh/americanexperience/features/pill-us-food-and-drug-administration-approves-pill/.

69 **"a bodily given on which":** Judith Butler, *Bodies That Matter* (New York: Routledge, 1993), 6.

70 **public was taboo:** Steven Pinker, "Sex Ed," *New Republic*, February 14, 2005, https://newrepublic.com/article/68044/sex-ed.

70 **Cisgender men and women—who make up:** Leonard Sax, "How Common Is Intersex? A Response to Anne Fausto-Sterling," *Journal of Sex Research* 39, no. 3 (2002): 174–78; B. D. M. Wilson and I. H. Meyer, "Nonbinary LGBTQ Adults in the United States," The Williams Institute, UCLA School of Law, June 2021.

70 **significantly greater physical strength:** Tia Ghose, "Women in Combat: Sex Differences May Mean an Uphill Battle," *LiveScience*, December 7, 2015, www.livescience.com/52998-women-combat-gender-differences.html.

70 **à la Judith Butler:** Olivia Goldhill, "Scientific Research Shows That Gender Is Not Just a Social Construct," *Quartz*, January 8, 2018, https://qz.com/1190996/scientific-research-shows-gender-is-not-just-a-social-construct.

72 **forty-two days after delivery:** Anita Slomski, "Why Do Hundreds of US Women Die Annually in Childbirth?" *JAMA* 321, no. 13 (2019): 1239–41.

72 **required child-support payments:** Belinda Luscombe, "How Deadbeat Are Deadbeat Dads, Actually?" *Time*, June 15, 2015, https://time.com/3921605/deadbeat-dads/.

72–73 **The COVID-19 pandemic exposed:** Women did three times as much unpaid childcare as men; women outpaced men in leaving the workforce and have been less likely to return. Shera Avi-Yona, "Women Did Three Times as Much Child Care as Men During Pandemic," Bloomberg, June 25, 2021, www.bloomberg.com/news/articles/2021-06-25/women-did-three-times-as-much-unpaid-child-care-as-men-during-covid-pandemic; Jonathan Rothwell and Lydia Saad, "How Have U.S. Working Women Fared During the Pandemic?" Gallup, March 8, 2021, https://news.gallup.com/poll/330533/working-women-fared-during-pandemic.aspx.

73 **In one groan-inducing:** Claire Cain Miller, "Nearly Half of Men Say They Do Most of the Home Schooling. 3 Percent of Women Agree," *New York Times*, May 6, 2020, www.nytimes.com/2020/05/06/upshot/pandemic-chores-homeschooling-gender.html.

73 **In contrast, a study:** "Male Birth Control Study Killed After Men Complain About Side Effects," NPR, March 11, 2016, www.npr.org/sections/health-shots/2016/11/03/500549503/male-birth-control-study-killed-after-men-complain-about-side-effects.

74 **their child was conceived:** Lawrence B. Finer and Stanley K. Henshaw, "Disparities in Rates of Unintended Pregnancy in the United States, 1994 and 2001," *Perspectives on Sexual and Reproductive Health* 38, no. 2 (2006): 90–96.

74 **"Having a child would mean":** "I Didn't Know What to Expect When I Got an Abortion," The Everygirl, January 13, 2020, https://theeverygirl .com/i-didnt-know-what-to-expect-when-i-got-an-abortion.

76 **introduced the term *biological clock*:** "The Clock Is Ticking for the Career Woman," the *Washington Post* declared on the front page of its Metro section on March 16, 1978, headlining an article by Richard Cohen, https://www .washingtonpost.com/archive/local/1978/03/16/the-clock-is-ticking-for -the-career-woman/bd566aa8-fd7d-43da-9be9-ad025759d0a4/.

76 **The average forty-year-old:** Ariana Eunjung Cha, "The Struggle to Conceive with Frozen Eggs," *Washington Post*, January 27, 2018, www.washington post.com/news/national/wp/2018/01/27/feature/she-championed-the-idea -that-freezing-your-eggs-would-free-your-career-but-things-didnt-quite -work-out/.

76 **"male fertility decline with age":** "Male Fertility Decline," Extend Fertility, July 18, 2018, https://extendfertility.com/male-fertility-decline/.

77 ***Cosmopolitan* magazine outlined:** Elizabeth Kiefer, "The No-Bullsh*t, Not-Scary, Actually Helpful Guide to Egg Freezing," *Cosmopolitan*, July 14, 2021, www.cosmopolitan.com/health-fitness/a36718692/egg-freezing-tips -cost-faqs/.

77 **The success rate of egg freezing:** "Egg Freezing: What's the Success Rate?" BBC, February 17, 2020, www.bbc.com/news/health-51463488.

77 **The majority of IVF cycles:** Anna Louie Sussman, "The Women Who Empty Their Savings to Freeze Their Eggs," BBC, June 28, 2018, www.bbc .com/worklife/article/20180627-the-women-who-empty-their-savings -to-freeze-their-eggs.

79 **A survey of 1,600 people:** Leonard Sax, *Why Gender Matters: What Parents and Teachers Need to Know About the Emerging Science of Sex Difference* (New York: Harmony Books, 2017), 38.

79 **an open relationship:** Jamie Ballard, "A Quarter of Americans Are Interested in Having an Open Relationship," YouGov America, April 26, 2021, https://today.yougov.com/topics/relationships/articles-reports/2021/04 /26/open-relationships-gender-sexuality-poll.

80 **When college students were asked:** Paula England and Jonathan Bearak, "The Sexual Double Standard and Gender Differences in Attitudes Toward Casual Sex Among US University Students," *Demographic Research* 30, no. 46 (2014): 1331.

80 **predictor of women's sexual enjoyment:** Elizabeth A. Armstrong, Paula England, and Alison C. K. Fogarty, "Accounting for Women's Orgasm and Sexual Enjoyment in College Hookups and Relationships," *American*

Sociological Review 77, no. 3 (June 2012): 435–62, https://doi.org/10.1177/0003122412445802.

80 **Forty-two percent of college men:** England and Bearak, "Sexual Double Standard and Gender Differences."

81 **when sex hurts:** D. Herbenick, V. Schick, S. A. Sanders, M. Reece, and J. D. Fortenberry, "Pain During Intercourse," *Journal of Sexual Medicine* 12 (2015): 1040–51, https://doi.org/10.1111/jsm.12841.

82 **earlier in life than men:** Anna Rotkirch et al. "Baby Longing and Men's Reproductive Motivation," *Vienna Yearbook of Population Research* 9 (2011): 283–306, www.jstor.org/stable/41342814.

82 **and more urgently:** Maja Bodin, Lars Plantin, and Eva Elmerstig, "A Wonderful Experience or a Frightening Commitment? An Exploration of Men's Reasons to (Not) Have Children," *Reproductive Biomedicine & Society Online* 9 (2019): 19–27, https://doi.org/10.1016/j.rbms.2019.11.002.

82 **In survey after survey:** Anna Brown, "1. A Profile of Single Americans," Pew Research Center, August 20, 2020, www.pewsocialtrends.org/2020/08/20/a-profile-of-single-americans/.

87 **Girls write long and detailed:** David Graeber, *The Utopia of Rules: On Technology, Stupidity, and the Secret Joys of Bureaucracy* (New York: Melville House, 2014).

90 **"Trauma and tragedy—the circumstances":** Martha Nussbaum, "Victims and Agents," in *The Art of the Essay*, ed. Philip Lopate (New York: Doubleday Anchor Books, 1999).

Chapter 5: Sex Is Spiritual

96 **One Catholic priest suggested:** Mike Mariani, "American Exorcism," *Atlantic*, December 2018, www.theatlantic.com/magazine/archive/2018/12/catholic-exorcisms-on-the-rise/573943/.

96 **Witness the Oregon father:** Hazel Cills, "Oregon Father Beats Up College Official over Daughter's Rape Case," *Jezebel*, December 18, 2019, https://jezebel.com/oregon-father-beats-up-college-official-over-daughters-1840506483.

96 **"I mean . . . violence is not":** OnlyJudyCanJudgeMe, December 18, 2019, comment on Cills, "Oregon Father Beats Up College Official."

97 **"It especially concerns affectivity":** Catechism of the Catholic Church (Vatican City, Italy: Libreria Editrice Vaticana, 1994), sec. 2332.

98 **"an expression of the holiness":** Rebecca Epstein-Levi, "Is Judaism 'Sex Positive'? Understanding Trends in Recent Jewish Sexual Ethics," *Journal of the Academy for Jewish Religion* 10 (2019): 15.

98 **"Have I not taught":** Thanissaro Bhikkhu (Geoffrey DeGraff), *The Buddhist Monastic Code: The Patimokkha Training Rules Translated and Explained* (Valley Center, CA: Metta Forest Monastery, 1994), www.nku.edu /~kenneyr/Buddhism/lib/modern/bmc/intro.html.

99 **Even *Teen Vogue* has endorsed:** Lisa Stardust, "How to Use Sex Magic to Manifest Your Best Self," *Teen Vogue*, June 25, 2021, www.teenvogue.com /story/how-to-use-sex-magic-to-manifest-your-best-self.

99 **"embodied spirits, inspirited bodies":** Margaret A. Farley, *Just Love: A Framework for Christian Sexual Ethics* (London: Bloomsbury, 2008), 123.

101 **"In a normal vita sexualis":** Sigmund Freud, *Selected Papers on Hysteria and Other Psychoneuroses* (New York: Journal of Nervous and Mental Disease, 1912), 188.

102 **"experts in the fields":** Eva Illouz, *Why Love Hurts* (Cambridge, UK: Polity Press, 2012), 45.

104 **The apostle Paul:** Sarah Ruden, *Paul Among the People: The Apostle Reinterpreted and Reimagined in His Own Time* (New York: Pantheon Books, 2010).

104 **Paul's description of humans:** Christopher Paolella, "'Neither Slave, nor Free, Male or Female?': Classical and Christian Conceptions of Slavery and Gender, and Their Influence on Germanic Gaul," *Journal of the Western Society for French History* 43 (2015), http://hdl.handle.net/2027/spo .0642292.0043.001.

105 **"Sex," as the philosopher:** Roger Scruton, "Bring Back Stigma," *City Journal*, Autumn 2000, www.city-journal.org/html/bring-back-stigma-11807.html.

107 **"Bad sex can leave you":** Ella Dawson, "'Bad Sex,' or the Sex We Don't Want but Have Anyway," *Elle*, December 12, 2017, www.elle.com/life-love /sex-relationships/a14414938/bad-sex-or-the-sex-we-dont-want-but-have -anyway/.

109 **"[A] woman or man who experiences":** Robin West, "Consent, Legitimation, and Dysphoria," *Modern Law Review* 83, no. 1 (2020): 1–34, https://doi .org/10.1111/1468-2230.12489.

Chapter 6: Our Sex Lives Aren't Private

113 **"hero women dating":** Kyle O'Brien, "'Single, Not Sorry': Tinder Swipes Right on First Brand Campaign from W+K," *The Drum*, October 8, 2018, www.thedrum.com/news/2018/10/08/single-not-sorry-tinder-swipes -right-first-brand-campaign-wk.

115 **edge of that shift:** Michael J. Rosenfeld, Reuben J. Thomas, and Sonia Hausen, "Disintermediating Your Friends: How Online Dating in the United States Displaces Other Ways of Meeting," *Proceedings of the National Acad-*

emy of Sciences 116, no. 36 (2019): 17753–58, www.pnas.org/content/116/36
/17753.

118 **"Of the desirability":** Samuel D. Warren and Louis D. Brandeis, "The Right to Privacy," *Harvard Law Review* 4, no. 5 (1890): 193–220.

120 **a private language:** Stewart Candlish and George Wrisley, "Private Language," in *The Stanford Encyclopedia of Philosophy*, edited by Edward N. Zalta, Fall 2019 edition, https://plato.stanford.edu/archives/fall2019/entries /private-language/.

124 **"Seeking to 'free' sexual love":** Wendell Berry, *Sex, Economy, Freedom & Community: Eight Essays* (New York: Pantheon Books, 1994).

126 **"The one central and indispensable":** Alan Jacobs, untitled post, *Snakes and Ladders*, February 25, 2019, https://blog.ayjay.org/placeholder-for-further -reflection/.

130 **simply personal preference:** Remember when John Mayer told a *Playboy* interviewer that he couldn't date Black women because he had a "white supremacist penis"? Elaborating further, he said that he had "a Benetton heart and a fuckin' David Duke cock." Later, he had the entire interview scrubbed from the internet. Latoya Peterson, "It's Impossible to Have 'a Benetton Heart' and a 'White Supremacist Dick,'" *Jezebel*, February 11, 2010, https://jezebel .com/its-impossible-to-have-a-benetton-heart-and-a-white-5469484.

Chapter 7: Some Desires Are Worse Than Others

135 **"we're less likely to judge":** L. M. Sacasas, "Ill with Want," *Convivial Society* 2, no. 13 (July 17, 2021), https://theconvivialsociety.substack.com/p/ill-with-want.

140 **abuse, and sexual dysfunction:** Dawn M. Szymanski, Lauren B. Moffitt, and Erika R. Carr, "Sexual Objectification of Women: Advances to Theory and Research 1ψ7," *Counseling Psychologist* 39, no. 1 (January 2011): 6–38, https://doi.org/10.1177/0011000010378402.

141 **"One wonders what has happened":** Rhiannon Lucy Cosslett, "Why Are So Many Women Writing About Rough Sex?" *Guardian*, February 7, 2019, www.theguardian.com/commentisfree/2019/feb/07/women-writing-rough -sex-metoo.

142 **"That isn't the whole":** Roger Scruton and David Edmonds, "Sex and Perversion," *Ethics Bites*, January 28, 2008, http://media-podcast.open.ac.uk /feeds/ethics-bites/transcript/ethicsbites6.pdf.

142 **"I . . . almost came":** *Girls*, season 1, episode 2, "Vagina Panic," directed by Lena Dunham, written by Lena Dunham, Lesley Arfin, and Sarah Heyward, aired April 22, 2012, on HBO.

144 **"in turn shapes":** Katherine Angel, *Tomorrow Sex Will Be Good Again: Women and Desire in the Age of Consent* (New York: Verso Books, 2021).

144 **"autonomy in general"**: Ellen Willis, *No More Nice Girls: Countercultural Essays* (Hanover: University Press of New England, Wesleyan University Press, 1992), 8.

145 **"an attitude towards human sexuality"**: Kate Shkodzik, "What Does Sex Positive Mean?" Flo.health, May 24, 2019, https://flo.health/menstrual-cycle /sex/pleasure/what-does-sex-positive-mean.

145 **"that prioritizes personal agency"**: Carina Hsieh, "What Does 'Sex Positive' Mean?" *Cosmopolitan*, December 25, 2019, www.cosmopolitan.com /sex-love/a30317658/sex-positive-meaning/.

145 **"Being sex positive means"**: Lacey Johnson, "Here's What It Really Means to Be Sex Positive," *Oprah Daily*, November 27, 2019, www.oprahdaily.com /life/relationships-love/a30028506/sex-positive-meaning/.

147 **"The 'I'm O.K., you're O.K.'"**: Ellen Willis, "Lust Horizons: Is the Women's Movement Pro-Sex?" *Village Voice*, June 1981.

148 **At *Slate*, an interview**: Shannon Palus, "The Ethical Cannibals of the World Would Like the Armie Hammer News Cycle to End, Too," *Slate*, January 28, 2021, https://slate.com/human-interest/2021/01/human-cannibals -armie-hammer-explained.html.

148 **"The problem is not that"**: Nicole Froio, "Whatever His Kink, Armie Hammer Is an Abuser," Bitch Media, January 20, 2021, www.bitchmedia.org/ar ticle/armie-hammer-cannibal-jokes-hide-abuse-allegations.

151 **tried to choke them**: Debby Herbenick et al., "Feeling Scared During Sex: Findings from a U.S. Probability Sample of Women and Men Ages 14 to 60," *Journal of Sex & Marital Therapy* 45, no. 5 (2019): 424–39, www.tandfonline .com/doi/full/10.1080/0092623X.2018.1549634.

151 **A BBC survey the same**: "BBC 5 Live, Women's Poll—21st November 2019," Savanta ComRes, accessed September 14, 2021, https://2sjjwunnql41 ia7ki31qqub1-wpengine.netdna-ssl.com/wp-content/uploads/2019/11/Final -BBC-5-Live-Tables_211119cdh.pdf.

151 **"But choking during sex"**: Dan Savage, "Savage Love," *The Stranger*, September 8, 2020, www.thestranger.com/savage-love/2020/09/08/44437066 /savage-love.

151 **Nonfatal strangulation is one**: Nancy Glass, Kathryn Laughon, Jacquelyn Campbell, Carolyn Block, Ginger Hanson, Phyllis Sharps, and Ellen Taliaferro, "Non-Fatal Strangulation Is an Important Risk Factor for Homicide of Women," *Journal of Emergency Medicine* 35 (2007): 329–35, https://doi .org/10.1016/j.jemermed.2007.02.065.

152 **"I never asked a boy"**: Peggy Orenstein, *Boys & Sex* (New York: HarperCollins, 2020), 44–45.

154 **When false information**: Karen Dill-Shackelford, *How Fantasy Becomes Reality: Seeing Through Media Influence* (New York: Oxford University Press, 2009).

154 **College students who consume:** E. Martellozzo et al., "I Wasn't Sure It Was Normal to Watch It," NSPCC Learning, 2016, https://learning.nspcc .org.uk/research-resources/2016/i-wasn-t-sure-it-was-normal-to-watch-it.

154 **Men who watch porn:** Neil Malamuth, Tamara Addison, and Mary Koss, "Pornography and Sexual Aggression: Are There Reliable Effects and Can We Understand Them?" *Annual Review of Sex Research* 11 (2000): 26–91, https://pubmed.ncbi.nlm.nih.gov/11351835/; Elizabeth Oddone-Paolucci, Mark Genius, and Claudio Violato, "A Meta-analysis of the Published Research on the Effects of Pornography," in *The Changing Family and Child Development,* ed. Claudio Violato, Elizabeth Oddone-Paolucci, and Mark Genius (London: Routledge, 2000).

154 **Women who consume it:** Susan M. Shaw, "Men's Leisure and Women's Lives: The Impact of Pornography on Women," *Leisure Studies* 18, no. 3 (1999): 197–212, https://doi.org/10.1080/026143699374925.

156 **"distortions of oppression":** Amia Srinivasan, *The Right to Sex: Feminism in the Twenty-First Century* (New York: Farrar, Straus and Giroux, 2021), 95.

Chapter 8: A New Ethic

161 **person and not oneself:** David Konstan, "Aristotle on Love and Friendship," *Schole* 2, no. 2 (2008): 207–12.

164 **"When you meet someone new":** Leah Libresco Sargeant, "The Risks of Sex," *Other Feminisms,* June 24, 2021, https://otherfeminisms.substack.com /p/the-risks-of-sex.

165 **"The consent question is absolutely":** Elizabeth Bruenig, "A Better Sex Ethic," *Medium,* November 9, 2017, https://medium.com/@ebruenig/a-better -sex-ethic-19e0e55a0e4e.

167–68 **"The Yes Means Yes law is":** Ezra Klein, "'Yes Means Yes' Is a Terrible Law, and I Completely Support It," *Vox,* October 13, 2014, www.vox.com /2014/10/13/6966847/yes-means-yes-is-a-terrible-bill-and-i-completely -support-it.

Chapter 9: Rethinking Sex

173 **"[Virginity] is a strange":** Jia Tolentino, "Interviews with a Virgin: Maya," *The Hairpin,* September 27, 2012, www.thehairpin.com/2012/09/interview -with-a-virgin-maya/.

174 **"I don't want to end up":** Jia Tolentino, "Interviews with a Virgin: Ben," *The Hairpin,* January 9, 2013, www.thehairpin.com/2013/01/interview-with -a-virgin-ben/.

174 **"Not having erotic capital":** Jia Tolentino, "Interview with a Virgin: Bette," *The Hairpin*, April 15, 2013, www.thehairpin.com/2013/04/interview-with -a-virgin-bette/.

175 **"not only what we *cannot*":** Rachel Hills, *The Sex Myth: The Gap Between Our Fantasies and Reality* (New York: Simon & Schuster, 2015).

175 **"The policing of sex":** Masha Gessen, "When Does a Watershed Become a Sex Panic?" *New Yorker*, November 14, 2017, www.newyorker.com/news/our -columnists/when-does-a-watershed-become-a-sex-panic.

177 **"We can starve to death":** Emily Nagoski, *Come as You Are: The Surprising New Science That Will Transform Your Sex Life* (New York: Simon & Schuster Paperbacks, 2015).

177 **"This great sex experience":** Sophie Lewis, "Collective Turn-off," *Mal* no. 5, July 2020, https://maljournal.com/5/sex-negative/sophie-lewis/collective -turn-off/.

177 **success in long-term relationships:** Olga Khazan, "Fewer Sex Partners Means a Happier Marriage," *Atlantic*, October 22, 2018, www.theatlantic .com/health/archive/2018/10/sexual-partners-and-marital-happiness /573493.

178 **adults profess to want:** Mark Regnerus, *Cheap Sex: The Transformation of Men, Marriage, and Monogamy* (New York: Oxford University Press, 2017), 174.

180 **"When I started my column":** Amanda Erickson, "'People and Their Problems Are a Renewable Resource': Dan Savage and Dear Prudence on Advice Giving and Sex," *Washington Post*, March 18, 2015, www.washingtonpost .com/posteverything/wp/2015/03/18/people-and-their-problems -are-a-renewable-resource-dan-savage-and-dear-prudence-on-advice-giving -and-sex.

182 **critic Hephzibah Anderson:** Hephzibah Anderson, "My Year Without Sex! Hephzibah Anderson Took a Dramatic—and Liberating—Decision. So Did It Help Her Find Real Love?" *Daily Mail*, June 26, 2009, https://www .dailymail.co.uk/femail/article-1195344/My-year-sex-Hephzibah -Anderson-took-dramatic--liberating--decision-So-did-help-real-love.html.

183 **"My instinct tells me":** Katherine Dee, "#52: What Is the Value of Restraint?" *Default Wisdom*, January 28, 2021, https://defaultfriend.substack .com/p/52-what-is-the-value-of-restraint.

187 **"I started to realize chastity":** Nellie Bowles, "These Millennials Got New Roommates. They're Nuns," *New York Times*, May 31, 2015, www.nytimes .com/2019/05/31/style/milliennial-nuns-spiritual-quest.html.